Edible Florida

By Don Philpott & Noreen Corle Engstrom

Acknowledgements

To Green Deane whose enthusiasm is infectious and whose knowledge is truly awesome.

Our special thanks to Amy Copeland for her illustrations on the inside covers; and to Alice Bard for reviewing the manuscript. Both are District Biologists with the Florida Park Service based out of Wekiwa Springs State Park.

Must Read Warning & Disclaimer.

This book is not intended to treat any medical conditions or health issues. The herbal uses listed are ones that have been documented in literature, both medical and non-medical, around the world. Many of the uses have traditionally been used by Native Americans and others for centuries. The reader must not try any of these herbal uses without first discussing them with their medical and health care providers.

The authors cannot be held in any way liable if the reader does not follow these instructions.

ALWAYS seek permission first if you want to forage on private land. It is **illegal** to forage on state park lands.

NEVER hunt critters without a permit or license if one is required and NEVER out of season.

NEVER hunt critters that are protected. States often have different rules so check with that state's wildlife commission or similar body.

Introduction

There are some 1.4 million known plant species worldwide and probably as many more as yet undiscovered. About 250,000 of these known species are edible of which about 170 species are cultivated globally. However just 12 of these species – grains, members of the grass family - provide around 75% of the world's food.

In Florida we are blessed with a climate that provides a year-round supply of wild foods – from tender leaves that can be used in salads or cooked as greens to nuts, seeds and berries for trailside snacks and roots that can substitute for potatoes or be ground to produce flour in the same way that the first Floridian settlers, the Paleo-Indians, did thousands of years ago.

Foraging food for free can be fun if you want to add some interesting and nutritious ingredients to your meals or need a handy trail-side snack. It is different from foraging in an emergency when your ability to find food could save the lives of you and your family. However, knowing what to forage for is a skill that will enhance your appreciation of and enjoyment in the countryside and is something you can do as a family.

You can supplement your kitchen supplies if you know the right things to pick from nature's abundant free larder. If you are camping you can add exciting new ingredients to your cooking and if you are under the weather, nature has a remedy to combat most ills.

We are not advocating the wholesale destruction of everything edible in the countryside but with a little thought and a little more knowledge there is no reason why foragers and campers should not only know more about nature but let it work for them as well. Leaves, berries, nuts and fruits can be picked but plants should not be uprooted or destroyed in the process. Exercise special care when harvesting roots to ensure the plant will survive.

Gather only what you need and never so much that the plant will die. A living plant can be a constant supply of food year after year. The only exceptions to this rule are invasive plants, especially exotics, that shouldn't be there in the first place. Forage away to your heart's content.

The rule is, of course, don't pick anything unless you are absolutely sure of what it is and know that it is safe. If in doubt, leave it alone. A plant that is safe for one person might cause an allergic reaction in another – simply touching the leaves could be enough to trigger it. If you are eating a plant for the first time that you know is edible, caution is still necessary. Try a little bit first to see if you are allergic to it. If not, tuck in. In this way you can build up a list of the plants that you know you can eat safely. Remember that even though a plant is edible, too much of it might be a bad thing. Many wild plants, such as wood sorrel, contain oxalic acid which is harmful if consumed in large quantities, but oxalic acid can be found in similar concentrations in many everyday household plants such as rhubarb and spinach. The moral is 'eat everything in moderation'.

There are hundreds of shrubs and plants to be harvested and enjoyed. Many are also highly nutritious. Young tender nettle leaves can be cooked and eaten as spinach. Chickweed, with its small yellow-green leaves, is rich in iron and can be eaten raw, added to salads or cooked. Grass seeds make a great trail snack. Yarrow, one of the most common of all wild flowers, can be boiled and eaten as a green vegetable. In olden days, couples getting married carried a bunch of yarrow because it was supposed to ensure lasting happiness. Shepherd's purse, sow thistles and plantain also make excellent green vegetable stand-ins. Wild herbs add flavours such as balm, peppergrass, rosemary and rue, are all found in the wild.

Everyone knows the dangers of eating poisonous toadstools but there are many varieties of edible fungi to add to the cook pot and some that can turn a meal into a feast. The huge horse mushrooms are tastiest when picked and dropped straight into the pan although they can be eaten raw when young in salads. There are numerous other fungi which can be eaten although generally, they have to be boiled for some time and their texture is nothing like a mushroom. You can boil turkey tail mushrooms in milk with some chopped onions to tenderize them.

If you are near the coast, edible seaweeds make delicious vegetable accompaniments and wild herbs can spice up any meal. Seaweeds are at their best when picked during the summer months. There are shellfish and fish - if it is legal to take them. Shellfish can be eaten all year round although it is best to avoid them during very hot weather. Only gather living specimens, wash well and cook quickly. You can tell if it is alive by trying to open the shell - if it is alive, it will quickly shut it again. If the shell is open or does not close, leave well alone. Shellfish are found almost everywhere along our shores but their breeding beds can be difficult to find – usually between the high and low water mark. Florida's inland waterways and lakes provide freshwater molluscs while freshwater crayfish can be harvested from the mud along the banks of rivers and streams.

Wild strawberries while small are delicious as are wild plums. Other fruits such as wild apples may not be as sweet but they are still nutritious – and free.

Late summer and autumn provides rich pickings with nuts, berries and other fruit. There are nuts for snacking and chestnuts to roast in the campfire.

Nature's larder truly is abundant and the more trees and plants that you are able to recognize, the more pleasure you will get from your trips into the countryside especially if you return to the same areas a lot. You may be out camping in the spring and recognize a walnut tree or spot a dense thicket of brambles or blueberries. Make a note because when you come back in the autumn there will be nuts and berries for the picking.

For centuries, wild plants and herbs have been used to treat ailments in the countryside and some of these remedies can still be very useful today. The leaves of blackberries for instance can be used to treat diarrhea, dandelion leaves are a natural diuretic and plantain leaves – chewed to soften them up – can be rubbed on insect bites to relieve the swelling and pain. The resin from the pine tree when mixed with a little sand can make an effective temporary tooth filling. Beautyberry leaves provide a natural insect repellant while dog fennel can relieve the itching from bites and poison ivy rash.

In our description of each plant we have listed the medicinal benefits that have been associated with it, often for centuries. When we write that it is used "to treat" a particular condition, we are relying in part on our own experience but far more on the wealth of scientific literature on the subject from around the world. The medicinal and health-giving properties of plants have been known for thousands of years and this knowledge was mostly passed down by word of mouth. This knowledge was rarely written down so many other possible remedies and treatments are lost forever.

The information provided in this book is for guidance only and is not meant to be used to treat any medical or other conditions. Always seek medical advice about any plants you are considering taking as a herbal remedy before doing so.

The great outdoors provides a year-round abundant supply of free and nutritional food for those willing to explore it. Join us as we explore nature's edible larder.

Plant Identification

You don't have to be a botanist to forage but some botanical knowledge is very useful. It is also important to be able to recognize the plant throughout the year.

There is no point in being able to recognize a plant only by its flower if you want to forage for its leaves out of the flowering season. Some plants only grow in or near marshes while others prefer the shade of a forest canopy. Knowing where the plant grows and under what conditions will also help in identification and allow you to be more focused in your search for it.

It is a good idea to be able to identify the different parts of plant and to understand descriptions of them. For instance, leaves have distinctive shapes – wedge-shaped, triangular, and spear-shaped and so on. The edge of the leaf (the margin) can be smooth, toothed or lobed. Leaf arrangements on a stem can be simple, opposite, compound, alternate and so on. See the illustrations of leaf types and shapes on the inside front and back covers.

Being able to describe a plant using these characteristics is another aid to assist you in the field in making a positive identification.

Root structures can often tell us a lot about edibility. The main root structures are bulb, clove, corm, crown, rhizome, taproot and tuber. When split in half, bulbs like onions have concentric rings while corms which are similar in shape, have solid centers. Cloves, like garlic, separate into several pieces; taproots, like carrots, can be single-rooted or branched. Crowns look like old-fashioned mop heads just below the surface – asparagus is a good example. Tubers, like potatoes, tend to grow in bunches below the plant, while rhizomes are fleshy roots that creep out in all directions.

In the same way that leaves and roots differ, so do fruits, flowers, tendrils and so on. The more you learn about these differences the more accurately you can describe and identify the plants you see. The difference between an edible plant and a poisonous one could be as subtle as the color of the tiny hairs on the underside of the leaf.

Queen's Anne Lace, also known as wild carrot, which is edible can be confused with Water Hemlock, which is not although both are members of the parsley family. Queen Anne's lace has fine hairs on green stems while water hemlock has hairless, smooth stems with purple blotches or streaks. That is why you should always carry a magnifying glass (10x or 20x magnification) to check for positive identification markers.

There are also other differences i.e. water hemlock blooms spring to fall while Queen Anne's lace blooms in the summer, the former has multiple flower heads while the latter normally has a single flower cluster at the top of the stem.

This book deliberately does not cover edible plants that can easily be mistaken for poisonous ones. Our aim is to encourage you to forage for the very many easily identifiable plants and then, as you gain more experience and confidence, you can turn your attention to the others.

Foraging rules –
Remember: All plants are edible once!

Never ever put anything in your mouth unless you are absolutely certain what it is.

Always know what you are eating. Many plants look similar, some are safe while others are not. Even the same plant can have some parts that are safe to eat and others that are inedible or poisonous and even the same part of the plant might be safe to eat or not depending on the time of the year. Don't guess. Plants must pass all ID tests – never assume. See the Universal Edibility Test below. Also the same plant can vary from year to year depending on the conditions i.e. too much rain or too little, too much sun or not enough. That is why you have to be absolutely convinced that you have correctly identified a plant, not just from a single characteristic or because it looks sort of like the picture in the book.

People can react to eating plants in different ways. One person can eat a particular plant with no side effects while another may experience a range of reactions from nausea and diarrhea to cramps and headaches. For instance, if you are very sensitive to poison ivy it is advisable to avoid other plants in the same family i.e. sumac, mango and cashews.

If tasting a plant for the first time, eat just a little to see if you have any adverse reactions. If after several hours you have none, you can add that plant to your list of 'personal' edibles.

If making a tea, tincture, concoction or wash from a plant use it sparingly for the first time to see if you are allergic to it or have any adverse reactions.

Know what parts can be eaten raw and what needs to be cooked. Some plants are toxic when raw but safe when cooked.

If it looks old or smells strange, don't eat it. The smell test is important i.e. if it smells like almonds but isn't an almond it is probably naturally occurring cyanide so don't eat it. However, if it smells like onions, garlic and mint even though it is none of those, it is usually edible.

If it has milky or discolored sap, don't eat it. Sap could be latex (allergenic) or poisonous. One of few exceptions is Usnea which is referred to later.

Many wild plants contain **oxalic acid** which can cause a tingling in the mouth and in high quantities, a burning sensation which may lead to kidney damage. Baking, drying or roasting will often remove the oxalates.

As a general rule don't eat if it has spines or fine hairs, beans or bulbs, white or red berries, shiny leaves or umbrella flowers. There are, of course exceptions, but this is a good rule to follow until you get more knowledgeable.

Plants can have many edible parts some of which may not be available at the time you are foraging. However, keep a diary of these plants and their locations so that you can return later to forage from them.

If harvesting bark, strip it from branches rather than the tree trunk.

In an emergency use the touch/taste test (see below).

Not all edible plants taste very nice but they provide nourishment – that is the difference between **foraging for fun** and **foraging for survival.**

Universal Edibility Test

There are many plants throughout the world. Tasting or swallowing even a small portion of some can cause severe discomfort, extreme internal disorders, and even death. Therefore, if you have the slightest doubt about a plant's edibility, apply the Universal Edibility Test (UET) before eating any portion of it.

Only test a plant if it is abundant. There is no point in going through the whole process if there are only two or three plants available. Remember test each part of the plant separately according to the UET.

Even after successfully testing a plant, eat it in moderation until you know what effect it has on you. For instance, eating a lot of wild apples, especially on an empty stomach, is going to give you stomach cramps or worse.

1.	Test only one part of a potential food plant at a time.
2	Separate the plants into its basic components—leaves, stems, roots, buds, and flowers.
3	Smell the food for strong or acidic odors. Remember, smell alone does not indicate a plant is edible or inedible.

4	Do not eat for 8 hours before starting the test.
5	During the 8 hours you abstain from eating, test for contact poisoning by placing a piece of the plant part you are testing on the inside of your elbow or wrist. Usually 15 minutes is enough time to allow for a reaction
6	During the test period, take nothing by mouth except purified water and the plant part you are testing.
7	Select a small portion of a single part and prepare it the way you plan to eat it.
8	Before placing the prepared plant part in your mouth, touch a small portion (a pinch) to the outer surface of your lip to test for burning or itching.
9	If after 3 minutes there is no reaction on your lip, place the plant part on your tongue, holding it there for 15 minutes.
10	If there is no reaction, thoroughly chew a pinch and hold it in your mouth for 15 minutes. **Do not swallow.**
11	If no burning, itching, numbing stinging, or other irritation occurs during the 15 minutes, swallow the food.
12	Wait 8 hours. If any ill effects occur during this period, induce vomiting and drink a lot of water.
13	If no ill effects occur, eat 0.25 cup of the same plant part prepared the same way. Wait another 8 hours. If no ill effects occur, the plant part as prepared is safe for eating.

CAUTION

Test all parts of the plant for edibility, as some plants have both edible and inedible parts. Do not assume that a part that proved edible when cooked is also edible when raw. Test the part raw to ensure edibility before eating raw. The same part or plant may produce varying reactions in different individuals

Recap

To avoid potentially poisonous plants, stay away from any wild or unknown plants that have —

- Milky or discolored sap.

- Beans, bulbs, or seeds inside pods.
- Bitter or soapy taste.
- Spines, fine hairs, or thorns.
- Dill, carrot, parsnip, or parsley like foliage.
- "Almond" scent in woody parts and leaves.
- Grain heads with pink, purplish, or black spurs.
- Three-leaved growth pattern.

These are good general rules to apply when you are first foraging. By sticking to them you will have to forgo some edibles but you will also avoid many poisonous plants. As you gain more experience and are able to positively identify many more plants you will learn which of these rules can be broken safely.

General Rules

Fruits – single fruits on stem generally OK, blue/black berries OK, seeds from all grasses OK, aggregated fruits (raspberries etc.) OK.

Plants - All dollar-weed type plants OK. All plants that smell like mint, onion and garlic OK.

Almost all roots and tubers can be roasted and eaten or crushed for flour.

Some Common Plant Herbal Uses

Beautyberry – rub leaves on skin for effective insect repellent (bunches of lemon grass and dried cattails also act as insect repellant).

Dock leaves – cut leaves into strips and use as astringent bandage.

Dog fennel – rub on skin to stop itching from stings and bites.

Florida betony – infuse leaves in hot water for relief of headaches.

Hercules club – leaves infused in tea relieves toothache.

Spanish moss – infused in hot water produces anti-bacterial drink.

Turkey tail fungi – anti-microbial, anti-oxidant, anti-malarial.

Usnea – natural antiseptic.

Wild mint – chew or infuse leaves for antiseptic properties.

Willow twigs – chew young twigs to combat headaches (contains salicin. – ingredient in aspirin), tea made from inner bark reduces fever.

Yarrow leaves placed on wound stop bleeding.

Medicinal Preparations

Tea: Steep in hot water

Infusion: Soaking leaves and/or flowers in either hot or cold water. Cold infusions may need several hours.

Tincture: Plant extracts combined with alcohol (often vodka) left to stand in a jar for 2-3 weeks, with frequent shaking, before being strained and bottled.

Decoction: Usually refers to root, bark or seeds and involves slow simmering

Poultice: An external moist application applied to a wound or affected area i.e. rash. The poultice is prepared by crushing plant material to release saps and juices. In some cases the plant parts i.e. leaves can be chewed to soften and moisten them first.

Wash: A tea or infusion for external application.

Nutrition

The U.S.-based Sierra Club has calculated that you need two and a half times as many calories to gain 1,000 feet of elevation as you do to walk at sea level for one hour at 2 mph. For example, an adult, depending on weight, needs between 350 and 500 calories an hour to cover 2 miles over rough but relatively flat terrain. To cover the same distance in the same time but ascending to 3,000 feet that same adult would need between 850 and 1,250 calories.

Even if you are out walking for just a few hours during the winter months, you will need more energy just to keep the body warm. In very hot weather, your energy requirements may be fewer but your liquid requirements increase. Sweating from exertions can present problems that can lead to dehydration and hypothermia in the winter, and dehydration and heatstroke in the summer. In the summer, it may be just too hot. In winter, it may be because you need to wear several layers of clothing. It has been estimated that a walker carrying a 35-pound pack in difficult terrain in very hot weather can lose up to 1.75 pints an hour from perspiration and this is in addition to normal daily water loss of about 2.75 pints through breathing, sweating and urinating. If you sweat a lot it is important to change into dry clothes when you get the chance and whether you sweat a lot or not, it is vital to drink lots of liquids.

Plant Preparation

Many plants can be eaten raw – as trail snacks or in salads – while others must be cooked either to make them edible and/or palatable. Plants that are edible provide nutrients but may taste horrible. Plants that are palatable are enjoyable to eat, like wood strawberries. Unfortunately, very many plants fall into the edible and not the palatable category. However, there are ways to improve flavour and edibility.

One of the greatest leaps early humans made was when they started to cook their food. Cooked food is easier to digest and generally more palatable. That means you use less calories to digest the food than if it was raw. In a survival situation that is very important. It is better to cook your food and have a hot, easily digestible meal so that the calories you save can be better used on staying alive.

Soaking and boiling leaves, stems and buds can reduce bitterness and tenderize the plant. It can also reduce saltiness. Sometimes you have to boil twice, throwing away the water from the first boil. Tubers and roots can be roasted, boiled or baked and often taste better for it. Drying is a good way to remove oxalic acid, found in many plants, especially members of the Arum family.

Leaching is a centuries-old technique to remove bitterness especially in acorns. Crushed acorns are placed in a strainer and boiling water poured over them. Alternatively, the sieve can be immersed in cold running water.

Lots of plants can be eaten raw but many of them are better cooked. Grains and seeds can be eaten raw until they ripen when they become dry and hard. Then grind or boil them and use as flour. Young leaves and shoots can be eaten raw and added to salads. They are often rich in proteins, vitamins and minerals and low in calories. Older leaves tend to have more fiber and will have lost some of their goodness.

Use plants like redbay, wild garlic, wild mint and sea lettuce as natural flavorings to spice up other dishes and the sap from trees such as maples, birches, walnuts and sycamores as natural sweeteners. Very young leaves from the maple also make a natural sweetener.

If you have a glut of plants or berries, you can juice, freeze, sun-dry, pickle or dehydrate them.

Dehydrating

Dehydrating is easy and cheap, the product keeps well and it is great way of enjoying foods long after they have gone out of season. Simply add water, bring to the boil, simmer for a few minutes and eat.

You can dry fruits, vegetables and mushrooms to reduce bulk and give them an extended shelf life. Take them with you for healthy snacks or to add to soups, stews and other recipes when camping or enjoy at home.

Do It Yourself dehydrating is easy using either a conventional oven or a commercial dehydrator. Drying is an ancient form of preserving food by removing the moisture on which bacteria, molds and yeasts can grow. It also has the advantage that the food is reduced in size and is lighter.

A commercial dehydrator usually has several trays with heat and air flow controlled automatically. Unless you plan to do lots of dehydrating, however, save the expense and use the kitchen oven.

Large items like apples should be cut into thick slices. Smaller fruit and vegetables can be dried whole. You need a large baking tray for each shelf in your oven and each tray will hold up to 2 lbs of prepared produce evenly spread out. Make sure there is enough room for air to circulate freely around the food.

Place the trays in a pre-heated oven when the temperature reaches $150°$ F ($65°$ C). It is a good idea to use an oven thermometer. This initial heat drives the moisture from the food. When the surface of the food feels dry, reduce the heat to about $140°$ F ($60°$ C). This is the most critical phase because you don't want to over-dry too fast or the food will taste leathery. The final drying phase can take between five and eight hours. The oven door should be slightly open so that the moisture can escape and if the oven doesn't have a fan, use an electric fan in front of the open oven door to ensure good air circulation. Every 30 minutes or so, rotate the trays as temperatures vary in different parts of the oven, and turn the food occasionally to ensure it dries properly and does not stick.

Once dried and cool, the food can be frozen in sealable plastic bags. Gather fresh produce when it is abundant. If you want to use the dehydrated produce in a recipe, simply add water and let it reconstitute. A good rule of thumb is one and a half cups of water for each cup of dried product. Don't add too much water or the product will go mushy. If it needs more water, you can add it judiciously during the soaking process.

Edible and Traditional Herbal Plants

Adam's Needle or Yucca

Yucca filamentosa

Where to look: Prairies, sand hills, grasslands, light woodlands and coastal dunes.

Identification: Rosette of sword-shaped leaves with threads on edges and clusters of drooping waxy, white-creamy colored bell-like flowers with six petals.

Edibles: Fruit and young flower spikes, seeds and young stems.

Fruit eat raw (bitter) but better baked or roasted. Roast seeds and grind, then boil until tender. Eat petals raw and add to salads. Flowers have a soapy taste which is removed by boiling. Peel and chop young stems and boil.

Cautions: If raw, eat small quantities of fruit and petals at first to see if they agree with you.

Medicinal: An infusion of crushed roots is said to treat headaches. Applied externally it treats head lice. Used as a poultice it treats sprains and sores. Soak roots and leaves in water to give a natural 'soap'.

Almond (tropical)

Terminalia catappa

Where to look: From Central Florida south in low-lying coastal areas.

Identification: Grows on average 30-50 feet tall but can be higher, with long spreading branches growing parallel to the ground and short-stemmed, foot-long, wide leaves and unmistakable large fruit – up to three inches long with shiny, waxy skin. Both leaves and fruit change color through the year from green to yellow to red.

Cautions: Fruit, leaves and bark contain tannic acid so don't overindulge.

Edibles: Fruit and husk can be eaten raw – best when young. Can be dried.

Medicinal: Leaves and bark are astringent. May have antioxidant properties.

Amaranth

Amaranthus viridis   *Amaranthus australis (Southern)*

Where to look: Prefers to be in or near freshwater and brackish wetland habitats.

Identification: An herbaceous annual that can grow to 10-15 feet tall but is usually much smaller with thick stems. It has alternate, oblong, pointed leaves with red-purple spots and red flower clusters.

Cautions: None

Edibles: Young leaves and growing tips, seeds. Eat young leaves and tips raw. Cook older leaves as spinach substitute (it has the same nutritional value). Seeds are highly nutritious and rich in protein, vitamins and minerals. Can be eaten raw or used as a gluten-free flour.

Medicinal: Leaves are astringent. Infusion of leaves can be drunk to treat diarrhea or gargled for mouth and throat problems.

American Beautyberry

Callicarpa americana

Where to look: Thickets, hedgerows and ground that is shaded.

Identification: Grows to six feet. Large, simple, opposite leaves with serrated edges. Very small flowers white to pinkish blue and clusters of small violet to purple berries.

Cautions: None

Edibles: Berries, roots, root bark and leaves.

Berries can be eaten raw but have little flavor although they do contain vitamins. They can be infused for a tea or to make jelly.

Medicinal: Squeeze the leaves to break the surface and then rub on skin to repel insects. Leaves have at least four chemicals that act as insect repellents. Berries also contain antioxidants. Infuse the roots for a tea for stomach ailments and dysentery and simmer root bark to produce a diuretic.

American Burnweed

Erechtites hieraciifolia

Also known as fireweed, pilewort and dog weed. One of the first plants to emerge after a burn.

Where to look: Wasteland, disturbed areas, water's edge – likes moist soils but very adaptable.

Identification: An erect annual that grow to nine feet with grooved, unbranched stem, topped with clusters of small pale yellow-white flowers enveloped in green bracts, lance-shaped alternate toothed leaves and an unmistakable aroma.

Cautions: Strong aroma and flavor.

Edibles: Young leaves, stems and flower buds can be eaten raw or cooked. Older leaves boil as greens.

Medicinal: An astringent. Whole plant infused for tea for mucous-coughs and colds, stomach ailments. Can be applied externally to relieve muscle pains.

Arrowhead, Broad-leaved

Sagittaria latifolia

Other names: wapato, duck potato

Where to look: Common aquatic plant found in lakes, ponds and waterlogged areas. You have to get wet foraging in the mud for the tubers. If you try to pull the plant out the tubers will snap off.

Identification: Leaves on long stalks resemble large pointed arrowheads with two long rear-pointing lobes. Leaves can vary enormously in length (from 3 inches to 3 feet) and width (less than inch to more than a foot). Flowers are white with three petals in whorls of three. A green seed ball develops in the center of the flower. As this ball turns brown it falls apart releasing the tiny, floating seeds. Potato-like tubers resemble slightly flattened spheres with a single shoot at one end. They grow on root runners in the mud. The bigger the plant the larger the tubers.

Cautions: Some other species of arrowhead may cause skin irritation.

Edibles: Tubers - can be eaten raw but much better prepared, peeled and cooked – roasted, boiled or steamed - as potatoes. Can also be dried and used for flour. Rhizome tips can be eaten raw or cooked. Young leaves can be cooked as a green. Petals can be eaten raw, taste like marshmallows.

Medicinal: A tea of young leaves was used to combat rheumatism pain and a tea from chopped tubers was used to combat indigestion. Root poultice for sores and wounds.

Bee Balm or Oswego tea
Monarda didyma

Member of the mint family

Where to look: Wood, thickets and along river banks. Likes moist soils.

Identification: Perennial that can grow to five feet tall but is usually half this size. Has square stem with paired, opposite, pale green, toothed lance-shaped, aromatic leaves and distinctive bright scarlet flower heads (whorls) and bracts. Fine hairs on both stem and leaves.

Cautions: None.

Edibles: Young leaves and florets. Young leaves and florets can be eaten raw, or the leaves cooked and added to other dishes for 'mint' flavoring. A tea made from 15-20 florets produces a full-flavored, refreshing drink.

Medicinal: An antiseptic, diuretic and stimulant. Infuse 3-5 fresh or dried crushed leaves (about one teaspoon) for a refreshing tea. The tea also treats colds, headaches and gastric disorders and flu by inducing sweating. A hanging bunch of leaves will make house/tent smell nice.

Beggarticks or Spanish Needles

Bidens alba

Where to look: Gardens, roadside, fields and disturbed habitats.

Identification: An herbaceous annual growing up to three feet with lobed leaves arranged oppositely with 3 to 5 leaflets. Small white daisy-like flowers with five petals. Bidens means 'two-toothed' which describes the points on the tip of the seeds. These catch on clothing and fur to aid seed dispersal.

Edibles: Tender shoots, petals and young leaves.

Young leaves and petals can be eaten raw. Older leaves can be boiled or steamed. Dried leaves can be used as a tobacco-substitute. Flowers can be infused for a drink.

Cautions: The plant contains many chemicals that have biological activity so should not be used medicinally without expert advice.

Medicinal: As a tea can be used to treat colds, fevers, flu and bacterial infections. Leaves were chewed for sore throats. Believed to have anti-inflammatory and antibacterial properties.

Blackberry

Rubus pensilvanicus (A member of Rose family)

Also called brambles. Not the same as black raspberry.

Where to look: Open ground with lots of sun and moist soils.

Identification: a woody perennial shrub that sends up red or green canes, flowers (in the second year) then fruits and dies. Grows to six feet or more often forming dense thickets. White flowers have five petals, leaves are serrated. Fruit unmistakable – go from white to red to blackish-blue when fully ripe.

Cautions: Prickles (not thorns) that can tear clothing and flesh.

Edibles: Berries and leaves, young shoots.

Preparation: Eat berries raw or preserve. Peel young shoots and add to salads or boil. Makes good wine, jelly, fruit tea.

Medicinal: Tea made from leaves or roots treats diarrhea. It is one of nature's wonders that eating too many berries can give you diarrhea while drinking a tea made from the leaves or roots can stop it. Fruit rich in vitamins C & K and manganese.

Blackroot

Pterocaulon pycnostachyum

Where to look: Pine flatwoods and sandhills. Likes sun.

Identification: A deciduous perennial herb that grows to about two feet. Has one or more striped (actually leaf wings) stems; stems and underside of leaves have white wooly hairs. Simple, alternate long narrow leaves with prominent white mid rib. Creamy flower clusters at top of stem form a spiky inflorescence or spiciform. It gets its name from its black, thick roots which produce a black sap.

Cautions: High tannin and contains coumarin which is an anti-coagulant. **Take in very small doses.**

Edibles: rhizome in small quantities for tea.

Medicinal: Plant contains antioxidant and anti-viral compounds which were used to treat colds and pulmonary illnesses. Fresh root is an emetic/laxative. A root tea was also used ease menstrual cramps.

Blueberry, Shiny

Vaccinium myrsinites

Where to look: Pine flatwoods, thickets and sandy uplands.

Identification: Squat bushes normally one to two feet high with alternate leathery, minutely-toothed leaves. It has clusters of reddish flowers and the ripe berries are blue or black.

Cautions: None.

Edibles: fruits and leaves. Fruit can be eaten raw, dried, used for jam or juiced. They freeze well. They are an antioxidant and a rich source of vitamins A and C. Leaves can be infused for a tea.

Medicinal: An infusion of berries treats diarrhea. An infusion of dried, crushed leaves treats nausea.

Blue Porterweed

Stachytarpheta jamaicensis

Where to look: Anywhere from sandy habitats to pine uplands. It can also be found close to streams and rivers.

Identification: A low growing bush with opposite, oval-shaped, dark green toothed leaves and five-petaled small blue flowers on long spikes.

Cautions: None

Edibles: Petals can be eaten raw – texture and taste of portabella mushrooms – or added as a flavoring. Good trail snack or add to salads. Infuse leaves for tea or beer.

Medicinal: Anti-oxidant. Tea from leaves used as a tonic and blood-cleanser.

Brazilian Pepper

Schinus terebinthifolius

Where to look: Invasive, aggressive exotic introduced as an ornamental plant called 'Florida Holly' – although not from Florida and not a holly. Likes disturbed areas, pinelands and mangrove forests but can be found in most terrestrial and aquatic habitats.

Identification: A broad leaved evergreen. Grows up to 30 feet tall with trunk hidden by thick layers of branches and a dense canopy that blocks sun to other plants. Alternately arranged oval and finely toothed reddish leaflets. White flower clusters and clusters of fruit that turn from green to bright red.

Cautions: Same family as poison oak and poison ivy so people with sensitivity to these may also be susceptible to Brazilian pepper. Treat with extreme caution until you know whether you are susceptible or not.

Edibles: Seeds and dried berries are used as a spice. Avoid the fruit.

Medicinal: It has antiseptic, antibacterial and antifungal properties. Research has found that bark extract is toxic against staphylococcus so may have a role to play in fighting fungus and harmful organisms.

Broomweed, Common Wireweed or Sida

Sida acuta

Where to look: Pinelands, hammocks and disturbed sandhill areas.

Identification: A perennial, long lived small, erect shrub with slender branched stems. Alternate, elongated, yellowish-green, toothed leaves with pointed tips on hairy stalks. Pale yellow flowers with five petals and five sepals. Fruit breaks into 5-8 wedge-shaped segments when mature.

Cautions: contains the alkaloid ephedrine so may react with some medications or if you have certain medical conditions, especially heart, thyroid conditions or diabetes.

Edibles: Leaves. Dried as a stimulating tea or boiled as a vegetable.

Medicinal: Decoction of sida roots and ginger is used to treat fever. Seeds are used to treat urinary infections. In the tropics it is used to treat malaria. Its antimicrobial properties have been used to treat skin infections.

Buckthorn, Silvery Buckthorn or Silver Bully

Sideroxylon alachuense

Where to look: Likes calcareous sandy and moist soils - hardwood hammocks, shell middens.

Identification: A now rare deciduous evergreen tree that grows to 25 – 30 feet with thorny stems and crooked branches and small, lustrous green alternate, simple elliptical leaves. Upper surfaces dark green, underside covered with silvery hairs. Tiny white flowers in clusters at the base of spur shoots. Shiny black oblong fruit (each a single berry).

Cautions: Thorns. Don't eat unripe fruit.

Edibles: Berries and seeds. Only eat raw berries when fully ripe.

Medicinal: Anti-inflammatory. A tea from the bark acts as a laxative while infusing the twigs and fruit produces an emetic.

Cabbage Palm, or Sabal Palm,

Sabal Palmetto

The Sabal Palm is the State Tree of Florida – even though palms are not trees but members of the grass family.

Where to look: Woods, marshes and hammocks. Likes sandy soils and can withstand occasional flooding.

Identification: A hardy, slow growing palm (20 – 50 feet tall) with an unbranched trunk covered with a criss-cross pattern of old leaf bases (boots) and large fan-like leaves growing straight from the top of the trunk and spreading out.

Leaves have up to 80 leaflets each an inch or more wide. It has clusters of small creamy flowers that hang from the crown on an inflorescence followed by small black fruit (drupes).

Cautions: None.

Edibles: Roots, very young leaves, growing (terminal) bud (cabbage or hearts of palm) and fruit sucked off the seeds.

Young leaves can be eaten raw or boiled. Heart can be eaten raw or boiled, steamed or fried. Seeds can be dried and crushed into a coarse inferior flour.

Medicinal: None known.

Caesar weed

Urena lobata

Where to look: Disturbed areas, pastures, edges of woods.

Identification: A small shrub with single stem from the ground which then has multiple branches. Young stems covered in tiny star-shaped (stellate) hairs, older stems are woody. Alternate gray-green, shallow lobed, ovate leaves with toothed margins and usually broader than long. Flowers clustered or solitary, have five pink petals on short stalks in the upper leaf axils. Fruit capsules have hooked spines and contain five barbed seeds.

Cautions: None known.

Edibles: Leaves raw or cooked. Sandy, chewy texture either way but a good survival food.

Medicinal: Roots are used as a diuretic. Infusion of root applied for rheumatism and lumbago pains. Infusion of flowers used to gargle for sore throats and as an expectorant.

Camphor

Cinnamomum camphora

Where to look: Likes open, sunny areas with well-drained soils.

Identification: A fast growing tall evergreen tree (up to 100 feet) with large, alternate, simple, ovate three veined leaves – dark green above, lighter on the underside. Young leaves are reddish and gradually turn green. Crush the leaves to smell the camphor. Tiny scented yellow flowers. Fleshy red round berries.

Cautions: Use in moderation – all parts toxic in large quantities.

Edibles: Leaves, shoots. Boil young leaves and young shoots. Dry older leaves and use as a spice.

Medicinal: Antimicrobial and analgesic. Oil from the bark used externally to treat fungal infections, and to relieve pain and itching. It is applied on the chest for coughs and an infusion of leaves and bark when added to water steam can be inhaled to relieve congestion and coughs. Internal use is not advised.

Camphor wood repels moths and many other insects.

Canadian Horseweed or Canada Fleabane

Conyza canadensis

Where to look: Fields, meadows, prairies and disturbed ground. Likes rich, moist soil with lots of sun.

Identification: A tall plant (up to seven feet) with a hairy, ridged stem and unstalked, slender, coarsely toothed, lance-shaped leaves up to four inches long with fine white hairs along the edges, which alternately spiral up the stem. Dense clusters of tiny flowers grow on multiple stems from the apex. Tiny greenish-white flowers grow on numerous flower stems at the top of the plant. Flowers have a ring of erect white or pink ray florets surrounding a yellow central disc.

Cautions: Some people get contact dermatitis after touching the plant.

Edibles: Young leaves and shoots can be boiled. Leaves can be dried, crushed and used as a seasoning (reminiscent of tarragon).

Medicinal: Antioxidant, antibacterial and antifungal. Tea from leaf used as a diuretic, astringent for diarrhea and to treat dysentery.

Catbriar, Common or Common Greenbrier

Smilax rotundifolia

Where to look: Woodlands, thickets, hedgerows. Likes moist soils.

Identification: A thorny, green thick stemmed climbing vine that uses aerial tendrils to latch on to other plants for support. Tendrils grow from lead axils. Alternate leathery glossy leaves are round to heart-shaped, parallel veined and smooth edged. Small flowers are greenish and fruit (berries) are also small and grow in clusters.

Edibles: Young shoots, growing tips, berries and roots (tubers). The above the ground part being harvested should snap off easily.

If it docs not it is too woody to eat. Raw shoots and tendrils have a slight nutty flavor. Young tips and shoots can be eaten raw. Young roots (i.e. still small) can be cooked (boiled or roasted), ground for a flour supplement or used as the basis for root beer. Berries can be eaten raw or cooked. Young fresh roots boiled make a refreshing tea.

Cautions: Thorns and prickles.

Medicinal: Anti-inflammatory. Root has been used to treat gout. Tea from stem for rheumatism and stomach ailments. Leaf poultice for boils. Poultice of leaves and stems used for rheumatism and muscle pains.

Cattails

Typha latifolia (wide leaf) and *Typha angustifolia* (thin leaf)

Where to look: Wetlands, ponds and damp areas.

Identification: Long flat, spear-like leaves and unique flowering spike that turns from green to brown.

Edibles: Young shoots and white growing tips on the rhizomes, stalk, flowers, pollen and roots (rhizome).

Young shoots can be eaten raw or boiled – tastes like asparagus. Pollen and roots can be used for flour. Pollen can also be added in equal parts to flour to give baked goods a yellowish-tint and very distinctive flavor.

Older leaves may be host to larvae of arrowhead beetle – also edible. Boil roots like potatoes but spit out fibers, or pound with water to remove starch and then grind and use as flour. The young female cattails can be boiled when green and eaten like corn on the cob. They taste like corn with a hint of olives.

Caution: Remove root fibers – can cause stomach upsets.

One acre of cattails produces about 6,500 lbs of flour a year. Provides water, food, shelter and heat. Brown flower heads can be used as kindling or ignited and held as a torch.

Medicinal: Dried cattails repel insects so hang a bunch on your porch or tent pole. Crushed roots in water can be applied to soothe sunburn. The ashes from burned cattail can be used on wounds –they stop bleeding and are antimicrobial.

Cedar, Eastern Red

Juniperus virginiana (a juniper not a cedar)

Where to look: Disturbed areas, oak barrens, prairies.

Identification: Pyramid-shaped, slow-growing evergreen tree usually growing to 60 feet with reddish brown, shredded bark and short opposite leaves in overlapping pairs. Young leaves are longer, needle-like and flat in whorls of three; older scale-like leaves overlap. Fragrant berries and leaves.

Cautions: A strong diuretic so use sparingly. Sharp leaves.

Edibles: Berries (modified cones) can be used for flavoring, as a spice, dried or used to make a drink.

Medicinal: Anti-viral, antibiotic, astringent and diuretic. Juniper berry tea for colds, bronchitis and stomach upsets. Poultice of powered leaves or oil used to treat warts and skin ailments. Tea from steeped leaves for sore throats and persistent coughs.

Chickweed

Stellaria media

Where to look: Likes moist soils. Waste and disturbed areas.

Identification: Ovate, smooth paired pointed leaves on hairy stems. The line of small hairs swap sides after each pair of leaves. Small white flowers with five petals shorter than the sepals.

Cautions: Mildly laxative

Edibles: Leaves, flowers, young stems and shoots. Winter crop (4-6 weeks season)

Raw in salads (has pleasant nutty flavor), boiled for five minutes like spinach or fried. It can be added as a flavoring towards the end of the cooking stage.

Medicinal: It has antibacterial, anti-inflammatory, expectorant and diuretic properties. The juice from crushed chickweed leaves can be applied as an antiseptic.

Tea from leaves is used as an internal cleanser and expectorant. Can be applied externally to prevent itching.

Note. Leaves fold up if it is going to rain.

Chinese Tallow

Sapium sebiferum

Where to look: Open fields, disturbed areas and grasslands.

Identification: A noxious, invasive, fast growing deciduous tree (usually about 30 feet) from Asia still sold as an ornamental. Often grows in stands. Has alternate, simple, ovate, smooth-edged, waxy bright green leaves (paler on the underside) which change to orange and red.

Clusters of small, individual white to yellow flowers in terminal, spiky inflorescence up to eight inches long. Three-lobed fruit, dark brown to black when ripe. When fully ripe the capsules open revealing three seeds covered in a white waxy coating. One tree can produce 100,000 seeds a year.

Cautions: Inner seed contains oil that is toxic to humans.

Edibles: Seeds have thick outer layer of edible wax that can be used in cooking like lard. Nectar produces a sought after honey.

Medicinal: Anti-viral. Poultice of leaves used for skin ailments and boils.

Waxy seed coating used to make soap and candles. The tree was introduced by Benjamin Franklin so that the wax coating the seeds could be used for candles. Wood cut into strips makes fragrant incense.

Coontie or Florida Arrowroot

Zamia pumila

Where to look: Well drained, sandy soils

Identification: A very slow-growing Cycad or "living fossil" which has been around since the dinosaurs. Looks like a small palm about two to three feet high with a subterranean stem. Colonies can be six feet wide. Long glossy dark green, leathery fern-like pinnate leaves (up to three feet long with narrow leaflets and cone-like fruits.

Cautions: It is a protected species so should not be foraged in the wild. Roots contain cycasin, a toxin, which is removed during correct starch extraction.

Edibles: Roots but never raw. Starch is extracted from grated, pounded root after several settlings in changes of water and then used as flour.

Medicinal: None known.

Coral Bean, Eastern

Erythrina herbacea

Where to look: Normally found along edges of bushy and open wooded areas.

Identification: Tall growing bush with arrow-shaped leaves in groups of three on thorny stems. It has distinctive long, narrow, tubular red flower clusters that can only be pollinated by hummingbirds.

Cautions: Thorns and the beans (bright red when ripe) in horseshoe-shaped pods are highly toxic.

Edibles: Flowers, young shoots and young leaves. Unopened flower buds and flowers can be eaten raw or added to salads. Young leaves, flowers and shoots can also be boiled for 10-15 minutes for a green leaf vegetable.

Medicinal: Rich in antioxidants. An infusion from the root was used for bowel pains and digestive problems. Decoction from leaves makes a reviving tonic.

Crabgrass

Digitaria sanguinalis

Where to look: In lawns, disturbed and waste areas, fields and pastures with other grasses. Likes sandy soils.

Identification: An annual, ground hugging, sprawling grass with spreading stems with wide flat leaves that lie on the ground with their tips pointing upwards. Spikelets are arranged in two rows and each has two florets.

Cautions: Some people are allergic to crabgrass.

Edibles: seeds

Toast seeds and grind for flour. It keeps well. Untoasted seeds can be used as rice substitute. It was one of the staple cultivated grains before corn. The seeds can be fermented to make beer.

Medicinal: Said to have emetic properties.

Creeping Charlie or Ground Ivy

Glechoma hederacea

Where to look: Lawns and damp, shaded areas especially pastures, woods and disturbed ground.

Identification: A perennial creeping plant with square stem that roots at the nodes with loose clusters of small blue-lavender flowers and round or kidney-shaped scalloped leaves.

Cautions:

Edibles: Boil young leaves and shoots as greens.

Medicinal: Infuse leaves raw or dried for an invigorating herbal tea.

Creeping Cucumber

Melothria pendula

Where to look: open woodlands, hammocks, thickets and hammocks.

Identification: a perennial vine with thin, smooth stem and alternate, slightly toothed, dark, green leaves that get smaller as they ascend. It uses tendrils to attach to other foliage and has small yellow flowers with five petals. Round, small dangling fruit turns from green to black when fully mature.

Cautions: Eat fruit when light green. Dark green and black fruit can have a strong laxative effect.

Edibles: Fruit is crisp and rich in carbs with good levels of protein and fiber. Although fruit resembles a very small apple or mini water melon it has a sort of cucumber taste. Eat young fruit raw or add to salads.

Medicinal: Laxative.

Creeping fig

Ficus pumila

Where to look: Moist to well-drained soils in areas that get lots of sun.

Identification: Woody, evergreen climbing shrub that grows to 12 feet or more with heart-shaped leaves. It attaches to other plants and structures with aerial roots. The leaves are very small in young plants and increase in size as plant matures. Fruit is pear-shaped and two to three inches long.

Cautions: None. Seeds are said to be toxic but I've not found evidence to supports this.

Edibles: Ripe fruit.

Squeeze fruit and cook strained juice then allow to cool into jelly or gelatin or add lemon for a drink.

Medicinal: Antioxidant and anti-inflammatory properties. Decoction of leaves for gastrointestinal issues

Crowfoot Grass

Dactyloctenium aegyptium

Where to look: Sandy to heavy damp soils, disturbed and open areas.

Identification: Stem creeps over the ground to form large mats of grass. Stem and leaves are smooth and hairless. Helicopter rotor-like flower head (with 2 – 7 spikes) on top of the stem. Seeds are on the underside of the spikelets. Plant gets its name because it was thought the spikelets resembled a crow's foot.

Cautions: Do not eat leaves or unripe seeds.

Edibles: seeds. Eat raw as trail snack or grind for flour or thickener

Medicinal: Stems and leaves used as a poultice to treat ulcers and wounds.

Dandelion

Taraxacum officinale

Where to look: Lawns, pastures, roadsides, disturbed areas.

Identification: Long, irregularly toothed leaves pointing away from the basal rosette. Hollow stems containing a milky sap. Distinctive solitary multi-petaled yellow flower on long stalk which becomes the downy white seed heads or 'blow balls'. Flower closes at night.

Cautions: Some people may get contact dermatitis because of the sap.

Edibles: All parts are edible. Young leaves and petals can be eaten raw. Larger leaves (more bitter) can be torn into pieces to remove the tough veins and boiled. The bitterness of the leaves can be offset in salads by using a vinegar-based dressing. Roots can be boiled as a vegetable (boil twice with a change of water) or roasted and ground as a coffee-substitute. The flowers can be dipped in batter and fried, infused to make a refreshing tea or used to make dandelion wine. Flower buds can be boiled or pickled. Infuse roots and leaves for a nutrient-rich tea.

Medicinal: Tea made from leaves can relieve constipation and tea from fresh roots aids digestion and is a diuretic. Root tea is also used for liver, kidney and bladder issues. The plant is a rich source of vitamins A and C and calcium.

Dayflower or white mouth dayflower

Commelina erecta

Where to look: Likes open pinelands, sandhills, dry scrub and woods but can adapt to most habitats.

Identification: An upright perennial plant that can grow to three feet with alternate, simple leaves and clusters of three-petaled flowers with lower paler petal smaller than two blue erect ones above. Lower petal also supports stamens. Heart shaped spathe below the flowers. Each flower only lasts one day – thus the name.

Cautions: Older plants have higher levels of oxalic acid which interferes with the absorption of calcium. Levels, however, are no higher than those found in chard.

Edibles: Roots, young leaves, young stems and flowers. Young leaves and stems can be eaten raw. Boil, steam or fry older leaves. Flowers can be eaten raw. Starchy roots can be roasted.

Medicinal: Diuretic. Tea from leaves used for colds and sore throats. The sap is used on skin irritations.

Dock, Swamp

Rumex verticillatus

Where to look: Forests with moist soils, swamps, marshes, riverbanks and floodplains.

Identification: Clusters of green flowers rise above the leaves which form a basal rosette. Petals are fused into a corolla tube.

Cautions: Maybe too bitter for some. Don't overeat.

Edibles: Leaves, inner stem and seeds

Young leaves can be eaten raw but are bitter (because of tannins and oxalic acid) so consumption should be moderate. It is best to steam or boil the leaves for 10-15 minutes to reduce the bitterness and then sauté them. Remove the midrib from older leaves. The flowering stems can be chopped up and boiled and the inner pulp then squeezed out. Seeds can be cooked.

Medicinal: The leaves are astringent and can be used as a bandage or you can press them into a poultice and apply to sprains or stings -i.e. nettle rash. The juice from crushed dock leaves can be applied as an antiseptic, and the juice from crushed roots treats diarrhea. A concoction from all the plant parts detoxes the body acting as a purgative.

Dollarweed or Pennywort

Hydrocotyle sibthorpoides. Also *H.umbellate* and *H. verticillata*

Where to look: Naturally moist areas or overwatered areas i.e. lawns.

Identification: A broadleaf plant that grows close to the ground with a single round leaf per stalk, like an umbrella. The leaf gets to the size of a silver dollar.

Cautions: Always wash thoroughly.

Edibles: leaves and stems. Eat raw or use in salads or as a potherb. Slightly bitter taste. Young leaves best. Leaves are less bitter than stems. Leaves can be fermented like kimchee.

Medicinal: Tea bitter but lowers blood pressure

Note: All plants with similar stem-leaf form are edible.

Ear Tree, Earpod Tree or **Elephant Ear Tree**

Enterolobium cyclocarpum

Where to look: Likes moist soils with sun. Pastures.

Identification: Tall trees (up to 105 feet) with thick trunk and huge, extending horizontal limbs and spreading, spherical crown. It has greyish bark with vertical reddish fissures. Long, alternate leaves with multiple thin leaflets (almost fern-like). Inflorescence of fragrant flower heads (up to 50) on long pedestals and green ear-shaped fruit pods that turn almost black as they mature. Protein-rich seeds have a reddish brown to orange ring.

Edibles: Seeds when ripe. Pith inside pod can be eaten raw or cooked. Seed pod should be dark brown and the seeds should rattle when you shake it. Ripe seeds can be boiled, roasted and eaten or ground for flour. Some people report having eaten young boiled seeds and lived to tell the tale.

Cautions: Don't confuse with *enterolobium contortisiliquum.* Both have ear-shaped pods but if the seeds can't be clearly seen and counted externally leave it alone. Edible seeds are round, inedible ones are pointed.

Medicinal: Extracts from bark used to treat colds and bronchitis.

Eastern Redbud

Cercis canadensis

Where to look: An understory tree in mixed forests, thickets and hedgerows. Likes moist soils and sun.

Identification: Can be large shrub or small tree with twisted trunk and spreading branches. Alternate, simple heart-shaped papery smooth-edged leaves with pointed tips, sometimes with hairs on the underside. Clusters of showy magenta pea-like flowers bloom before leaves burst. Seeds are contained in a brown, flattened pea-like pod two to three inches long.

Edibles: Young twigs used as seasoning. Flowers, flower buds and unripe pods can be eaten raw (great in salads) or sautéed. Seeds can be eaten raw or roasted. Flower buds can be pickled.

Cautions: None.

Medicinal: Tea from inner bark is astringent. Bark infusion used for fevers and diarrhea. Infusion of roots and inner bark for congestion and chest colds. Seeds contain antioxidants.

Eelgrass

Vallisneria Americana

Also called ribbon grass, wild celery.

Where to look: Freshwater streams, lakes and rivers and slightly brackish water. Eelgrass is a good indicator of water quality – it doesn't do well in polluted water.

Identification: This perennial plant roots in the river bed and sends up clusters of submerged, round-tipped, ribbon-shaped leaves from the root. Leaves have raised mid-ridge, are up to one-inch wide and can be several feet long. White flowers on long stems that break the surface. Male flowers develop at the base of the plant and break away when mature and float to the surface where its pollen is released. Banana-like fruit pods contains many seeds.

Cautions: None

Edibles: young leaves cooked.

Medicinal: None known.

Elderberry

Sambucus Canadensis

Where to look: Edges of woods or thickets. Likes wet or moist soils.

Identification: 5-11 tooth-edged leaflets, dense clusters of small white flowers in summer and purple black berries in the fall.

Edibles: Berries, blossoms, leaves and young shoots.

Eat berries when raw in small quantities (they contain glucosides). Infuse berries for tea or tincture or make into jelly. They can be cooked or dried after destalking. Dried they keep for many months and are easily reconstituted in water. Flower clusters can be dipped in batter and fried. Use berries and flowers for tea, wine and champagne. Soak flower heads in water for half a day, discard the flowers and you have a palatable drink.

Elderflower champagne - infuse about six flower heads in a gallon of water, add two sliced lemons, cover and let stand for 24-36 hours. Strain the liquid through a cloth; add 1 ½ lbs. of sugar and stir until dissolved and bottle. Use screw caps but don't put on tight. The liquid will have attracted wild yeasts and fermentation will start in the bottles. After one or two weeks, when the bubbles stop or are reduced to a slight trickle, tighten the screw tops and leave the liquid to carbonate for a few days. Serve chilled and you have a very refreshing, low alcoholic drink.

Cautions: Unripe berries can cause stomach upsets and diarrhea. DO NOT confuse with the toxic water hemlock. Elderberry has bark and opposite, compound leaves and berries. Water hemlock does not have bark, has alternating leaves, does not have berries and the stem usually has purple colorations.

Medicinal: Antibacterial. Glycosides break down to hydrocyanic (prussic) acid. An infusion of flowers reduces fewer and a tea from flowers and fruit treat colds, flu, asthma and arthritis.

Epazote

Chenopodium ambrosioides

Where to look: Waste and disturbed ground.

Identification: Short lived herb growing 2-3 feet, irregularly branched with oblong, toothed, lance-like leaves 3-4 inches long. Small green flowers grow from a branched panicle at the apex of the stem. Strong odor.

Edibles: Leaves and stems. Raw has a strong, mixed spice flavor. Two or three leaves can be added to soups, stews and fish dishes for added flavor. In Mexico it is widely used as a spice to flavor fish and bean dishes.

Cautions: Use essential oil in moderation. It is toxic.

Medicinal: A tea from leaves is a natural antiseptic and tonic and can help reduce fevers. Oil extracts are used to treat worms.

False Hawksbeard

Crepis japonica (also called Youngia japonica)

Where to look: Moist grassy areas, pastures, disturbed and waste land.

Identification: Member of the daisy family and like a mini-dandelion with rosette of heavily veined leaves with curled edges and a darker line round the margins. Small yellow flowers on long, branched stems.

Edibles: Young leaves can be eaten raw but older leaves, which may be bitter, are better cooked. Roots can be roasted and ground as coffee-substitute.

Cautions: None.

Medicinal: Antiviral, anti-inflammatory and may have anticancer properties. Infusion of crushed leaves can be applied to bites, stings and boils.

Fern, **Bracken**

Pteridium aquilinum

Cinnamon fern (*Osmunda cinnamomea*), Gold Leather Fern (*Acrostichum aureum*)   Giant Leather ferns (*Acrostichum danaeifolium*), Ostrich fern (*Matteuccia struthiopteris*), and Sensitive fern (*Onoclea sensibilis*) all have fronds that are edible before they uncurl.

Where to look: Woodlands, water's edge, damp soil terrain.

Identification: Large, coarse fern with highly divided erect, triangular leaves (fronds), noticeably three-forked, with multiple oblong leaflets. When the frond first emerges it is coiled up and hairy, resembling the head of a violin thus the name 'fiddlehead'. Can form large colonies.

Edibles: Young shoots best boiled twice. Can then be eaten as is, added to stews or quickly sautéed. Roots (rhizomes) can be dried for flour or used to make a beer-like drink.

Cautions: While some people do, it is not advisable to eat fiddleheads raw. They should also be consumed in moderation and not on a regular basis.

Medicinal: Root tea used for stomach cramps and diarrhea. Root poultice was applied to burns.

Fireweed or Pilewort, see American Burnweed

Florida Betony (Rattlesnake weed)

Stachys floridana

Where to look: Sunny areas with moist, well-drained soils.

Identification: Member of the mint family with hairy, upright, square stems. Grows up to two feet. Lance-shaped leaves are opposite, slightly toothed and have a blunt end. Small white to pink flowers are trumpet shaped growing in whorls in the lead axils.

Edibles: Roots, leaves, shoots and seeds. White, segmented tubers (like a rattlesnake's tail) can be eaten raw, added to salads, cooked or pickled. They are crunchy and prized as a delicacy overseas. They also have high water content. Young leaves and shoots can be cooked as greens. Use fresh or dried leaves as tea or tincture.

Cautions: None.

Medicinal: Antioxidant. Leaves reduce headaches. Roots contain stachyose, a sugar substitute that promotes good bacteria in gut and inhibits growth of bad bacteria. American Indians smoked leaves as tobacco-substitute.

Fragrant water lily

Nymphaea odorata

Where to look: Ponds and slow moving waters.

Identification: An aquatic perennial with large plate-like green leaves and showy, fragrant white flowers with pointed petals floating on the surface of the water.

Edibles: Young leaves, flower buds, seeds and rhizomes. The thick starchy rhizomes can be eaten after cooking. Seeds, rich in starch, can be boiled and ground for flour. Young leaves while still unrolling and flower buds can be boiled.

Cautions: Use in moderation.

Medicinal: Astringent, antiseptic and antispasmodic. Root tea for coughs and diarrhea and root poultice can be applied to swellings and sprains.

Gallberry, Inkberry and Appalachian Tea

Ilex glabra

Where to look: Pine flatwoods and open sandy areas.

Identification: A medium-sized shrub (up to six feet), spreading evergreen holly often with multiple trunks and branching twigs. It has thick, alternate, oblong evergreen leaves -shiny on top and lighter on the underside. Leaves are generally smooth with a few tiny teeth near the tips. Drupes (berries) turn from green to jet black when ripe.

Edibles: leaves. Roasted crushed leaves for decaf-coffee/tea type drink.

Cautions: Use in moderation.

Medicinal: Infusion of roasted leaves used as diuretic and stimulant.

Ginger, Wild

Asarum canadense

Where to look: Woods and moist, rich soil shady areas. Not strictly a Florida native but grows in Georgia and has been cultivated in Florida gardens and some has escaped.

Identification: A squat, creeping, colony-forming plant with distinctive large, satiny, heart-shaped paired leaves and solitary mauve-brown, hairy blossoms, often hidden and close to the ground, of three petal-like sepals. Horizontal fleshy roots (rhizomes).

Edibles: Root and leaves. Crushed root can be eaten raw or dried and used as a ginger-like flavoring. Leaves can be used fresh or dried. Roots can also produce a candy if boiled and then slowly simmered in sugar.

Cautions: Use in moderation. Some people may also be susceptible to skin irritation after contact with the plant.

Medicinal: Diuretic, expectorant and antiseptic. Root tea used for coughs, colds, sore throats and indigestion and poor digestion.

Glasswort, Perennial

Sarcocornia ambigua

Where to look: Salt lakes, salt marshes, close to the ocean.

Identification: A low growing, succulent branched plant with jointed, fleshy light green stems that may turn to red. Stems have a thin woody core which thickens as it ages. Tiny flowers.

Edibles: Tender stems. Eat raw in salads as a trail snack or pickle. Salty to the taste. Older stems, before they get too woody, can be boiled.

Cautions: None.

Medicinal: Juice from crushed stems used as a diuretic. Oil from ashes of the plant used as a soap.

Goldenrod, Sweet

Solidago odora

Where to look: Woodlands, pine habitats and disturbed ground

Identification: Perennial. Grows three to five feet. Clusters of small golden yellow flowers that look like plumes. Stems hairy. Lance-shaped leaves are slender, toothless, parallel veined and smell of anise when crushed. Hold the leaf up and you should see tiny transparent spots.

Edibles: seeds, shoots, leaves and flowers. Fresh and dried leaves for a refreshing tea. Batter and deep fry inflorescence

Cautions: Might cause an allergic reaction.

Medicinal: A tea from flowers acts as a mild diuretic and stimulant and was traditionally drunk to fight off colds. Poultice of dried leaves and flowers to stem bleeding.

Gopher Apple

Licania michauxii

Where to look: Dry, sandy habitats. Likes well-drained, sunny sites.

Identification: Low growing, ground covering shrub sometimes called ground oak because stiff, simple, alternate leaves look like bright green narrow oak leaves. Has yellowish clusters of five-petaled flowers. Fruit is one to two inches long with a single seed.

Edibles: Fruit. Eat raw. Opinions vary about taste – many people think it tastes like pink bubble gum.

Cautions: None known.

Medicinal: Infusion used for vomiting, stomach pains and diarrhea.

Grapes

Vitis aestivalis (summer grape), *vitis rotundifilia* (muscadine), *vitis labrusca* (fox grape)

Where to look: Well drained, sunny spots on the edges of woods and thickets.

Identification: Climbing, woody vines with large, coarsely toothed heart-shaped simple leaves with tendrils opposite. Greenish flowers and clusters of fruit from blue to purple black in color depending on species. Muscadine vines, which were here when the Spanish arrived, have a single leading tendril while fox grapes, the result of cross breeding with European varieties, has two leading tendrils. Fox grapes are more acidic.

Edibles: Young shoots and leaves of all species listed above are edible raw or cooked. Leaves can also be used to wrap foods for cooking to add flavor. Sap is edible raw. Grapes are rich in sugar when ripe but can be acidic. Eat raw, make into a drink, dry or use for jelly.

Grape vines are a good source of water. Cut the vine close to ground and place end in container. Make a second diagonal cut in the vine about five feet from the ground but don't go all the way through. Water will run from the cut end into the container.

Cautions: Don't overindulge on grapes

Medicinal: Grapes are diuretic, detoxicant and laxative and rich source of vitamins and essential minerals. Leaf tea used for diarrhea and stomach upsets and a leaf poultice for fever, headaches and rheumatism pains.

Greenbrier see **Catbriar**

Hackberry or Sugarberry

Celtis occidentalis

Where to look: Woods, hammocks, sites with dry to moist, rich soils.

Identification: Rapid growing deciduous tree (up to 70 feet but usually smaller) with cork-like 'warty' gray bark. Alternate, single, evenly serrated course, egg-shaped leaves with curved long leaf tips and uneven shoulders. Pea-sized purple-black fruit.

Edibles: Fruit (berries) including kernel. Eat raw when dark orange (at its sweetest), use in jelly or dry. Best berries are at top of tree, when over ripe they fall off the tree.

Cautions: None.

Medicinal: Extract from wood used to treat jaundice. Decoction from bark used for sore throats

Hercules Club (Toothache tree) , Southern Prickly Ash or Pepperwood

Zanthoxylum Clava-Herculis

Where to look: Dry, light sandy, well-drained soils, sunny areas – meadows, pastures, prairies.

Identification: Grows as small tree or shrub. Trunk and older branches covered with spiky, corky knobs (like little pyramids), young twigs, branches and leaf stems have thorns. Long, alternate, pinnately compounded, toothed, leathery leaves – glossy green above with paler underside - and multiple leaflets. Each small flower turns into a single seed bearing fruit. Flowers grow in dense clusters so fruit/seed gathering is easy. It is a member of the citrus family.

Edibles: More medicinal than edible although the seeds were used as a pepper-substitute.

Cautions: Always use in moderation.

Medicinal: Antibacterial and anti-inflammatory. Chewing leaves and bark or a tea from bark and leaves relieves toothache. It induces a numbing sensation in the mouth. Decoction from roots used to induce sweating. Fruit can be rubbed onto stings and itches for temporary relief.

Hickory, Pignut

Carya glabra

Where to look: Well-drained, sandy, sunny areas, slopes and dry, open woodlands.

Identification: Tall, deciduous tree with large canopy and alternate, pinnately-compound leaves with up to seven lance-like and serrated leaflets. The small, yellow-green drooping catkin-like flowers are wind pollinated. Nuts are in a four-valved, thin husk which partially breaks open when ripe. Gather when nuts fall to the ground.

Edibles: Nuts, sap, leaves. Nuts can be eaten raw or roasted. Can also be ground as flour. Soaking before cracking them open prevents pieces of shell flying everywhere. Sap can be boiled and reduced to syrup.

Cautions: None known.

Medicinal: None known.

Holly, Yaupon

Ilex vomitoria

Where to look: Moist sandy soils – woods, clearing and thickets.

Identification: Large, shrubby evergreen with long, alternate, oval, leathery, glossy, scalloped-edged leaves – dark green above and lighter on the underside. Has clusters of red berry-like fruit.

Edibles: Leaves. Roast and dry the leaves for a caffeine laced tea.

Cautions: Use in moderation.

Medicinal: The plant has been used in rituals by Native Americans for hundreds of years. A strong tea made from the leaves was used for purging before many rituals. A lighter infusion is said to help people sleep better. It also acts as a diuretic.

Hog Plum, also known as Tallow Plum, Tallow wood plum

Ximenia Americana

Where to look: Dry, sandy scrubby areas to hardwood hammocks.

Identification: A thorny tree that often does not grow larger than a large shrub. Oval-leaves that smell of almonds. Pale yellow, fragrant flowers with four petals. Almost round yellow to red, smooth-skinned fruit with yellow flesh.

Edibles: Cook young leaves as greens. Fruit, eat raw or cooked. Can be dried and made into jelly. Kernel is edible raw or cooked.

Cautions: Eat leaves in moderation. Raw leaves contain cyanide and too many cooked leaves act as a purgative.

Medicinal: Infusion of leaves and twigs is used to treat coughs and fevers and in more concentrated doses as a laxative. The bark is used to treat sore muscles.

Huckleberry, Dwarf

Gaylussacia dumosa

Where to look: woodlands and dry, open spaces. Likes acid soils.

Identification: Usually a small shrub. Similar to blueberry but has gold-like flecks on the underside of the leaves (you need a magnifying glass to spot them).

Edibles: berries - always 10 seeds to each fruit. Eat raw, dry (like raisins) or use for jellies and pies or press for a sweet drink. They can be fermented into wine. High in vitamins A, B and C and minerals, especially iron.

Cautions: Overindulgence can cause stomach upsets and diarrhea.

Medicinal: They are astringent, antioxidant and antiseptic. Native Americans ate the berries to increase their night vision. Fruit is said to improve the circulatory system and lower blood sugars and has been used to treat urinary tract infections. A tea from leaves may lower blood sugars and ease inflammation.

Hydrilla

Hydrilla verticillata

Where to look: in almost any fresh and brackish water.

Identification: An invasive exotic aquatic plant that forms dense, clogging mats unless treated or removed. It has small, saw-toothed leaves with a red midrib arranged in whorls along the stem which can grow to more than 20 feet. It has tiny flowers with three petals with red streaks and three sepals. It reproduces mainly vegetatively and one piece breaking away is enough to start a new plant.

Edibles: All green parts.

Wash very thoroughly, dry, crumble and add to soups, stews or salads

One of the richest plant source of calcium known (10-13%)

Cautions: None known.

Medicinal: A powder of dried, crushed hydrilla is used to treat cuts, ulcers and boils – it is said to speed healing.

Jack-in-the-Pulpit

Arisaema triphyllum

Where to look: Woodlands and thickets with moist soils.

Identification: An herbaceous long-living perennial that grows up to two feet tall with groups of three long leaves growing together at the top of the stem. Inflorescences are green to greenish-yellow with the often-striped spathe (the pulpit) wrapped round the spadix (Jack) wich is covered with tiny flowers. The fruit, scarlet when ripe, is clustered around the spadix.

Cautions: The plant contains calcium oxalate crystals (raphides) which can cause a burning sensation in the mouth so should not be consumed raw.

Edibles: Starchy root should be cut very thin, air dried (for 10-12 weeks) and then roasted or boiled. Can also be ground after drying as a flour.

Medicinal: Dried roots infusion used to treat coughs and colds. Dried roots also used as poultice for rheumatism and sores.

Kudzu

Pueraria lobata

Where to look: Edges of woods, thickets, waste and disturbed ground.

Identification: An invasive aggressive semi-woody vine from Japan that can grow 100 feet or higher. Large, oval alternate leaves in groups of three and downy on the underside. Purple-flowers have yellow patch on upper petal and smell strongly of grapes.

Cautions: None.

Edibles: Young leaves, flowers and unripe pods are edible raw or cooked. Leaves can be dried for a tea. Roots are rich in starch and used to thicken soups and sauces. Roots can be roasted as a vegetable. For flour, grate roots and soak in water. When the starch has settled on the bottom, carefully pour off the water, then recover with water and repeat. The starch can then be dried and crushed. Use as a flour, thickener or shape into 'noodles' which can be boiled.

Medicinal: Tea from root for headaches and gastro-intestinal problems. Tea can be gargled for sore throats. Tea from flowers to reduce stomach acid. Overseas seeds are used to treat dysentery.

Lantana

Lantana camara

Where to look: Waste, cleared and disturbed sunny areas.

Identification: Evergreen, perennial shrub (5-6 feet tall) in the verbena family, that can form dense thickets. It has hairy stem, long, textured, opposite, simple, toothed, hairy leaves. Crushed leaves smell like cat's pee. Clusters of small, tubular, multi-colored, four petal flowers at the stem ends. Flowers change colors after pollination.

Edibles: Berries -must be very ripe – almost black – can be eaten raw or used for jelly. Taste sparingly at first.

Cautions: Berries toxic when unripe. Leaves and berries contain a photosensitizing chemical which may make you more sensitive to light.

Medicinal: Antimicrobial and fungicidal. Tea from leaves used for colds, flu and fevers. Crushed leaves relieve itching. Leaves repel insects.

Lemon Grass

Cymbopogon citratus

Where to look: Well drained, moist, sunny areas

Identification: Tall (up to six feet), evergreen, perennial, fragrant grass growing in dense, spreading clumps. Long (up to three feet) narrow, belt-like, bluish-green leaves with dropping tips and sharp edges. Citrus aromas when crushed.

Edibles: Grass blades, lower white, fleshy stalks. Use chopped blades and crushed stalks as a flavoring in food. Use blades for lemon tea. Can be dried and powdered.

Cautions: Should be avoided if pregnant. Leaves have sharpish edges, thus its other name – barbed wire grass.

Medicinal: Antimicrobial and antifungal. Rub on skin as an insect repellant or hang bunches on back porch and at entrance to tent or RV. Rub crushed grass on scalp to relieve headaches. Leaves yield citral, the aromatic, essential oil. Inhaling the essential oil is used in aromatherapy for muscle pains. Strong tea from leaves relieves anxiety and aids sleep. Lemongrass oil is used in a number of pesticides.

Magnolia, Sweetbay

Magnolia virginiana

Where to look: Woodlands, lowlands, swamps

Identification: An evergreen tree (up to 90 feet although usually much shorter) with large, perfumed bowl-shaped creamy white flowers and alternate, simple, leathery, smooth leaves – shiny above with silvery underside. Has smooth, ash-gray bark. Younger stems covered with a white down which rubs off as the tree develops.

Edibles: Leaves, petals and bark. Use leaves as a bay leaf substitute and condiment, petals can be pickled and make great sweet and sour relish. Use sparingly as strong flavor.

Cautions: None.

Medicinal: Bark is an astringent and stimulant. Use tea from bark as anti-inflammatory and stimulant. A wash from the bark can be used on skin ailments, sores and itches. Use leaf tea for coughs, colds and as a tonic.

Maple, Red

Acer rubrum

Where to look: Like wet, moist soils in woodlands and near water.

Identification: Fast growing tree. Bark smooth and grey on young trees, scaly and darker on older trees. Large oval leaves with usually three (but could be up to five) gently toothed, pointed lobes. Red flowers and red twigs. Winged seeds.

Edibles: Inner bark, sap, seeds, leaves. Raw seeds can be bitter but can be boiled with two changes of water or roasted. The young leaves can be eaten raw or boiled. They contain sugar. Add a couple of just-burst leaves or sap to sweeten coffee or tea if you normally add sugar. Sap can be drunk straight from the tree or slowly boiled to make syrup. The inner bark can be eaten raw, boiled or roasted. Maples provide a year-round food supply.

Cautions: None known.

Medicinal: Bark is astringent. Infusion of inner bark used externally to treat sore eyes. Infusion of outer bark was used to treat cramps.

Marsh Pennywort or Water Pennywort

Hydroctyle umbellata

Where to look: Along water's edge or in shallow water.

Identification: Resembles dollar weed with a single terminal round notched leaf with singe cleft. Leaf is about the size of a half-dollar. Small light green, star-shaped flowers. Stem attaches to the center of the underneath of the leaf. It has creeping stems. Can grow in tangled colonies and become dense mats.

Edibles: Leaves can be eaten raw or cooked. Leaves less bitter than the stems.

Cautions: Forage in unpolluted spots and wash leaves thoroughly before eating.

Medicinal: Tea from leaves used to reduce anxiety.

Mexican Clover

Richardia brasiliensis

Where to look: Dry to mesic disturbed sites, gardens, orange groves

Identification: Member of the coffee family. Deep rooted small (four to five inches high) plant with branching stems and simple, opposite, oval or elliptical leaves with rounded to pointed tips. Inflorescence of multiple whitish, five petaled flowers (often 20 or more). The petioles of opposite leaves are connected by hairy sheath-like stipules

Edibles: Leaves eat raw or boiled.

Cautions: None known.

Medicinal: Antiemetic and antimicrobial. An infusion or decoction of root is used as an expectorant, antiemetic and diaphoretic (increases sweating).

Milkweed vine or white milkweed

Morrenia odorata

Where to look: Woods to tropical forests – anywhere where it can climb.

Identification: Perennial vine with long (five inch) deep green, paired leaves arranged like a five-armed starfish, with small greenish white five-petaled flowers.

Edibles: Everything above ground. Fruits year round. Young leaves, young shoot tips, flowers and young fruit can be eaten raw. Leaves and young shoots can also be boiled. Older fruit is best roasted and can be dried. The stalks can be boiled and peeled. Unripe seeds are edible but ripe seeds are not.

Cautions: Eat in moderation because of white sap and avoid if you are allergic to latex.

Medicinal: Sap can be applied on warts to remove them.

Mulberry, White and Red

Morus alba (white) *morus rubra* (red)

Where to look: Woods, likes rich soils

Identification: Small trees. Red mulberry has heart-shaped, fine-toothed leaves, rough above and hairy on the underside. White mulberry is hairless. Red mulberry fruit are like thin blackberries and turn from red to purple when ripe, the white mulberry bears white to purple fruit.

Edibles: Fruit and short young shoots.

Eat fruit raw, cook or press for high carb juice. Can be dried and kept. Young shoots can be boiled as a vegetable.

Cautions: Unripe fruit and raw shoots contain hallucinogens.

Medicinal: Red mulberry root tea was used as a tonic. Berries lower fever. White mulberry leaf tea for coughs and headaches.

Muscadine see Grape

Nakedwood Twinberry or Simpson's Stopper

Myricanthes fragrans

Where to look: Well-watered, exposed, sunny spots, scrub and coastal hammocks.

Identification: Grows as a large shrub or small tree with smooth, greyish bark which naturally peels to reveal orange-red underbark. Opposite, simple, ovate fragrant deep green leaves with rounded leaf apex and notched margin and pellucid dots. It has small, four petaled, fragrant white flowers with long stamens and the fleshy fruit (berry), often in pairs (i.e. twinberry), is orange to red when ripe. A member of the Eucalyptus family although the crushed leaves smell more like nutmeg.

Cautions: None known.

Edibles: Ripe fruit is edible raw and has citrus-like taste.

Medicinal: Was used to stop diarrhea.

Nettles

Urtica spp

Where to look: Waste, disturbed and open ground. Like the sun.

Identification: Often grows in dense clusters with a knotted mesh of narrow rhizomes below ground. Stems are hollow, square and have grooves running their length. Leaves are toothed with a pointed tip. Small green flowers grow in clusters from the leaf axils.

Edibles: Young shoots, leaves, roots.

Very young leaves can be eaten raw, boiled or quickly sautéed, which also removes the stinging hairs, and then served with butter and a squeeze of lemon. Older leaves should be gently simmered to tenderize. You can drink the cooking water. Leaves can also be added to soups. Rich source of protein, vitamins A and C, iron and other minerals.

Cautions: Use gloves when harvesting.

Medicinal: A nutritious tea from the leaves and stem can treat colds, flu and asthma. Dried leaves can be applied to wounds to stem bleeding. Research in Europe suggests that plant extracts might help people suffering from arthritis.

Nightshade, American Black nightshade or Glossy

Solanum americanum

Where to look: Waste and disturbed sites, open woods, roadsides.

Identification: Grows to three to four feet with wide branching stem which may appear purplish in the sun. Leaves are alternate (hairy on the underside), ovate with wavy margins and some coarse teeth. Small white, five lobed flowers with yellow stamens and shiny black berries (when ripe) with many seeds growing in a cluster with short stems connected to a longer common stem. The berries are green and speckled with white dots when immature.

Edibles: Fruit (must be very ripe) can be eaten raw or cooked for jelly and jams. Young shoots and young leaves should be boiled twice in different changes of water.

Cautions: Use only if you are 100 percent sure of your identification, otherwise leave well alone. Contain varying levels of the glycoalkaloids – solasonine, solanigrine and saponin.

Medicinal: An analgesic and sedative. Crushed leaves were applied externally on burns, sprains and swellings.

Oaks

Quercus spp.

There are many species of oak and they come in all shapes and sizes and all have acorns. They can be divided into two main oak groups – white and red. White oaks have acorns every year while red oaks bear acorns every other year.

Oaks, White

Live Oak

Examples: Live Oak - Quercus virginiana, Chapman Oak – sandhills, sand scrub dunes; Quercus chapmanii, Sand Live Oak – *Quercus germinate.*

Where to look: Live oaks – sandhills, sandy soils; Chapman oak - sandy scrub, dunes, sandy ridges; Sand live oak – oak scrubs, sand scrub, dunes.

Identification: White oak leaves don't have bristle tips (red oaks do). The nutshell which holds the acorn is smooth. Live oaks have evergreen leaves with rolled edges. Stigmas lack stalks. Upper tree bark is rough.

Edibles: Acorns, leaves if pest free. White oak acorns are less bitter than red oaks (they have less tannin). They can be roasted and eaten or crushed for flour or use as a coffee substitute. They can be eaten raw if sweet. Acorns are rich in protein and fat.

Cautions: Eat raw acorns sparingly – the tannin can cause stomach problems and will give you a headache.

Medicinal: Astringent and antiseptic. Infuse oak bark and acorns in boiling water to externally treat athlete's foot. Repeated applications may be necessary. The bark has a high tannin content and can be used to make a tea to treat mouth ulcers. A weak decoction of bark can be drunk to treat diarrhea and dysentery or applied externally to treat aching muscles and joints.

Oaks, Red

Quercus spp.

Examples: Turkey oak - *Quercus laevis*, Myrtle Oak – *Quercus myrtifolia*, Water Oak – *Quercus nigra*

Where to look: Turkey oak – sandhills, sand ridges, dunes; Myrtle oak – sandhills, sand dunes, sand ridges; Water oak – swamps, areas with wet or moist soils.

Identification: Red oaks have bristle-tipped leaves and the inside of the nutshell is usually hairy. Stigmas have stalks. Upper tree bark is smooth.

Cautions: See white oaks.

Edibles: Acorns, leaves if pest free. Red oak acorns are bitterer as they contain more tannin. This means they can be stored longer. In addition, red oak acorns are generally more plentiful than white oak acorns. Add wood ash to water and soak red oak acorns for several hours to remove bitterness. Change the water frequently. The acorns that sink are less bitter. Clean young leaves can be eaten raw as a survival food.

Medicinal: See white acorns.

Turkey Oak

Papaya

Carica papaya

Where to look: Likes rich, sandy well-drained soils and sun. Frost sensitive.

Identification: Grows palm-like up to 30 feet with very large, spirally arranged seven-lobed leaves at the top of the trunk. Small, waxy, splayed five-petaled flowers grow from the leaf axils and then become the large round to pear-shaped fruit. Flesh of fruit is orange when ripe.

Edibles: Fruit, flowers, seeds, pith and leaves. Eat fruit raw or cook. Boil young leaves, flowers and new growth stems, discard water and boil again. Old leaves need to be boiled in several changes of water. The juice from unripe fruits can be rubbed onto meat to tenderize it. Black seeds can be ground and used as a pepper-like flavoring. Stalk pith is edible raw. Rich in potassium and vitamin A.

Cautions: Milky juice may cause skin irritations. Contains the alkaloid carpain so prepare leaves correctly.

Medicinal: Antifungal and antimalarial. Flesh of fruit can be applied externally on cuts, ulcers, stings and burns.

Passionflower vine
Passiflora incarnata

Where to look: Sandy soils, disturbed ground and thickets.

Identification: A climbing, woody vine that grows to 30 feet and more with coiled tendrils and cleft, lobed, finely-toothed, leaves. Large, beautiful, light purplish flowers with pink threads, with fleshy, egg-shaped fruit (may pops) which turns from green to yellow as it ripens.

Edibles: fruit, flowers, leaves

The flowers make a stunning centerpiece for salads and can be eaten raw. Fresh yellow fruit can be eaten raw or squeezed for juice. Green fruit can be eaten raw but best cooked. Makes a delicate sorbet. Leaves are best parboiled and then sautéed.

Cautions: Because of sedative properties, it should be used in moderation.

Medicinal: Tea or tincture, Drink a tea of leaves and flowers for depression, anxiety, insomnia and muscle pains. It is also a mild diuretic and sedative. Poultice from roots for boils, cuts and swellings.

Pawpaw

Asimina obovata

Where to look: edges of fields, thickets, streams and woodlands

Likes sun and sandy soils.

Identification: Usually found as a shrub but can grow into a small tree. Has alternate, smooth-edged leaves, and large whitish-yellow flowers with maroon centers, that stink of rotting meat which attracts pollinating insects. Hanging fruit changes from green to yellow or brown as it ripens.

Edibles: Fruit

Eat fruit raw or baked. Fruit can be dried for storing. Don't eat peel or crush seeds (may cause stomach problems). Whole seeds should pass through without any issues. Vitamin rich (A & C).

Can be used as ice-cream flavoring and to make beer.

Cautions: Some people get a skin rash when handling the fruit. Some people get nauseous after eating the fruit.

Medicinal: Leaves are diuretic. Native Americans used dried seeds to control head lice. Fruits can be used as a laxative.

Pennyroyal

Piloblephis rigida

Where to look: Likes well-drained sunny habitats - palmetto scrub, sandhills, open woods and pine flatwoods

Identification: Restricted to Florida and a couple of counties across the border in Georgia. An aromatic evergreen perennial with low growing, stiff branches and dense, opposite, needle-like leaves. Rarely more than a foot tall. Distinctive white and mauve to purple flowers with five splayed petals, two up and three down.

Edibles: Fresh or dried leaves for a refreshing, mint tea (however, a little goes a long way so experiment with quantities until you get the taste you like) or add to soups and stews for flavor.

Cautions: To be avoided if pregnant.

Medicinal: An emetic. Tea from leaves for treatment of colds and fevers. A stronger tea can induce vomiting.

Pepperweed

Lepidium virginicum

Where to look: Waste and disturbed areas. Like dry soil and sun.

Identification: Racemes from the plant's highly branched stem look like a bottle brush. The racemes bear the tiny white flowers with four petals and then the round, flat green seedpods. Sessile, lance-like alternate leaves are larger near the base of the plant. Plant rarely more than twenty inches high.

Edibles: Young leaves can be eaten raw or boiled. All parts of the plant have a peppery taste and you can use young seedpods raw or cooked to add 'pepper' to your dishes. The root can be prepared and used like horseradish.

Cautions: May cause blistering and skin irritations.

Medicinal: Crushed leaves can be rubbed on poison ivy rashes. Poultice from root can be applied to reduce swelling of sprains. Leaf tea for coughs.

Persimmon

Diospyros virginiana

Where to look: Edges of woods, fields, meadows, trails. Likes sun.

Identification: Trees grow to 50-60 feet but in Florida rarely grow more than 10-12 feet tall. Dark bark in square patterns, stiff, shiny, oval pointed leaves, dark green above, lighter below. Flowers are greenish-white; fruit like large plums, orange to red when fully ripe.

Cautions: East in moderation as fruit is hard to digest.

Edibles: Fruit. Shake the tree and gather the ripe, soft fruit that fall to the ground. Edible raw when ripe and sweet, unripe fruit is very astringent. Fruit can be dried, used in jelly or ice-cream, used in bread or fermented into wine. Dried leaves make a vitamin C-rich tea. Seeds from fresh fruit can be roasted, ground and used as a caffeine-free coffee-type drink.

Medicinal: Inner bark is very astringent. Bark tea used for stomach aches.

Pickerelweed

Pontederia cordata

Where to look: Aquatic plant in swamps, ponds, shallow waters and mud flats.

Identification: Grow to about three or four feet. Large, broad, waxy arrow to lance-shaped leaves, thick fleshy stem topped by distinctive spikes of blue-violet flowers. Flowers most of the year.

Edibles: Flowers, young leafstalks and young leaves before they unfurl can be eaten raw or boiled. Fruit with a single seed can be eaten raw, roasted, dried or ground and used as flour. Seeds are ripe when they drop off in hand after a gentle shake of the plant.

Cautions: Some people may get an allergic reaction from eating the seeds.

Medicinal: An infusion was used by American Indians as a contraceptive.

Pine, Longleaf

Pinus palustris

Where to look: Sandy soil areas, sandhills,

Identification: An evergreen that grows to 90 feet and more. Needles up to 12 inches long, usually in groups of 3. Large cylindrical cones up to ten inches long. Each scale has a short curved spine.

Edibles: Inner bark and bark of young twigs (peel off outer layer), seeds, shoots, needles, pollen, sap and roots. Boil, bake or roast cones to get seeds. Throwing cones in the campfire will cause the scales to split open so the seeds can be extracted. Seeds can be eaten raw or cooked. Chew or infuse needles for tea - rich in vitamins A and C. Chew sap. Strips of inner bark can be eaten raw or fried or boiled as noodles or dried and ground for flour. Young pine roots stripped of their bark are also edible raw.

Cautions: Avoid large doses of sap – might cause kidney damage.

Medicinal: Inner bark is an expectorant. Infuse bark for herbal tea. Green pine needles provide a vitamin C rich tea. Pine resin applied to wound will stop the bleeding. Young pine cones are high in testosterone. Resin mixed with sand makes temporary tooth filling.

Resin can also be used on open wounds to speed healing. Pine needles contain shishimic acid (used in Tamiflu).

All pine trees in this region have the same edible parts as listed above.

Plantain, Southern

Plantago virginica

Where to look: Waste and disturbed ground and lawns.

Identification: Rosette of long basal oval to oblong leaves from which unbranched, leafless, hairy flower spikes develop. Spikes of tiny greenish white flowers. Leaves have parallel veins and hairy margins. Upper leaf surface is hairy, underside is downy.

Edibles: Young leaves can be eaten raw and added to salads, older leaves with ribs removed can be boiled as greens or added to soups. Old leaves are too stringy to eat. Young flowering spikes can also be eaten raw or sautéed.

Cautions: None known.

Medicinal: An astringent, expectorant and antimicrobial. Rub leaves on insect bites and stings and nettle rashes to ease the pain. Use poultice of leaves on boils and ulcers.Tea from leaves used as tonic, to aid healing and for chest congestion. Scientific studies suggest it might be useful in reducing cancerous tumors.

Poison Ivy

Toxicodendron radicans

Where to look: Woods, thickets

Identification: "Leaves of three, leave it be." A vine related to the cashew that has alternate, three pointed leaves on long stems. The two bottom leaves left and right and the third leading leaf is always the largest of the three. Leaves can be smooth edged or toothed. White flowers and clusters of drooping small white berries.

Edibles: Young leaves (if you are not susceptible to poison ivy) but not worth taking the chance.

Cautions: Some people have a strong allergic reaction to contact with poison ivy but many people are not susceptible to it. If you are in contact with poison ivy you want to wash the oil off your skin as quickly as possible. Splashing water on the affected area works, bathing the area with soapy water is better. Many people are affected after stroking their pets that have been in contact with poison ivy. The pets are not susceptible to it but they carry back the oil from the leaves on their fur.

Medicinal: Not edible but sap was used to get rid of warts. American Indians used to and many country folk still do eat the first poison ivy leaves that appear at the beginning of the growing season. They eat young leaves every day for 21 days by which time they have acquired a year's immunity from the plant.

Pokeweed

Phytolacca americana

Where to look: waste and disturbed ground.

Identification: A multi-branched coarse perennial with red stems and large oval, toothless leaves. Long stalked flower clusters. Flowers have five greenish-white petal-like sepals. Clusters of hanging deep purple berries.

Edibles: Young leaves, young shoots, fruit and stems. Boil leaves twice and dispose of water after first boil. Leaves rich source of vitamin C. Stems can be pickled when still green, avoid if purple. Berry fruits must be cooked.

Cautions: All parts poisonous if eaten raw. Leaves and shoots must be boiled in changes of water.

Medicinal: The root used in a decoction can be used to treat skin ailments such as eczema and fungal infections. Native Americans used a berry tea to fight dysentery, rheumatism and arthritis. A poultice from the roots for rheumatism, sprains and swellings. Research is ongoing into a leaf extract that might help fight cancers.

Prickly Pear

Optunia humifusa

Where to look: Dry, rocky and sandy well-drained areas with full sun.

Identification: Multiple segmented flattened green pads with spines and barbed hairs (glochids). Pads edged with large yellow waxy flowers and red, pulpy fruit.

Edibles: Eat fruit, flowers and peeled pads raw. Pads can be boiled, fried or dried. Roast seeds and crush for flour or thickener. Flowers can be cooked. Fruit can be cooked as a vegetable, pressed to make a drink or made into a preserve. Ripe pads are tasty and have a high water content so are a good rehydration source.

Cautions: Prickly pears have thousands of tiny barbed hairs all over the pads which will stick in your skin and hurt. Use thick gloves to peel them or a pair of tongs. Alternatively throw the pads into the campfire for a couple of minutes and let the flames burn the hairs off.

Medicinal: Flowers have astringent properties and can be used as a poultice on open wounds. A tea from the flowers treats diarrhea and irritable bowel syndrome. Split raw pads used as a poultice on burns, wounds and for rheumatism pain. Baked pads used externally on ulcers.

Purslane or Pigweed

Portulaca oleracea

Where to look: Rich, sandy soils, waste and disturbed areas, hedgerows.

Identification: Prostrate annual with smooth, reddish, forking stems and clusters of succulent, alternate spatula-shaped leaves at stem joints and stem ends. Small yellow flowers with five petals usually only opens for a few hours on sunny mornings.

Edibles: All parts are edible. Eat leaves and stems raw as trail food or in salads, boil or fry. Stems can be pickled. Seeds can be eaten raw or used as flour. Often called the 'world's most nutritious green', as leaves rich in vitamins A & C, iron, calcium, potassium, melatonin and magnesium and fatty acids (Omega 3)

Cautions: None known.

Medicinal: Antioxidant, antibiotic and diuretic. Juices from squeezed plant make an invigorating tonic or can be used externally as a poultice to treat minor burns, bruises and sores. Leaf tea for headaches and stomach aches.

Queen Palm, or Cocos Palm

Syagrus Romanzoffiana

Where to look: Prefers well drained, acidic soils with lots of sun.

Identification: Fast growing to about 50 feet with smoothish trunk and crown of pinnate 'fluffy' leaves up to 12 feet long. Older leaves turn brown and droop. Growth rings on the trunk are visible. Bunches of creamy flowers and seeds develop below the leaves. Ripe fruit (dates) is yellowy-orange and falls to the ground.

Cautions: When collecting fallen fruit ensure they are free from mold.

Edibles: Fruit. Wash thoroughly and then eat the sweet, sticky flesh but not the seed.

Medicinal: Antioxidant and astringent. Tea from fruit used for sore throats, colds and stomach pains. Crushed seeds used to treat fevers.

Ragweed, Common

Ambrosia artemisiifolia

Where to look: Likes sunny, waste and disturbed ground, roadsides.

Identification: Member of the aster family. Grows up to three feet off the ground with hairy stem and deeply cut, alternate leaves (although may be opposite) and long flower spikes with tiny green flowers.

Edibles: Protein-rich seeds can be eaten raw. Seeds also a rich source of oil which can be obtained by crushing and then boiling the seeds. The oil is scooped off as it rises and settles on the surface.

Cautions: Major cause of pollen-related allergies. Some people may get contact dermatitis from touching the plant.

Medicinal: Astringent antibacterial and antiviral. Crushed leaves take sting out of insect bites. Mild tea from leaves for fevers and nausea. Mild root tea for menstrual pains.

Reindeer Moss

Cladonia rangeferina, also check out C.evansii

Where to look: Open well-drained sandy scrubs with partial shade.

Identification: An ashy-gray colored, slow growing lichen (not a moss) that grows in ground hugging, multi-branched spongy clumps. All lichens are a symbiotic relationship between fungi and algae.

Edibles: All parts. Can be eaten raw as a survival food (is chewy and will give you severe stomach aid but provides protein, vitamins and minerals) but best soaked to remove acidity (bitterness). Can then be added to soups and other dishes. Crunchy, brittle texture. Dried and powdered, can be used as a flour-extender.

Cautions: Eating raw lichen can give you severe stomach ache. Lichens also absorb pollutants so choose collecting sites carefully.

Medicinal: Tea from boiled lichen used for diarrhea.

Note: Makes great kindling when dry

Rose, Sweetbrier

Rosa eglanteria, R. palustris is another Florida rose

Where to look: Road sides, clearings

Identification: Grows into a dense fragrant shrub up to six feet tall, with thorn covered curving stems. Pinnate leaves with ovate, double toothed leaflets with a serrated margin and hairs. Flowers in clusters have five pink petals with a white base and yellow stamens. The fruit is a roundish red hip.

Edibles: All parts. Flowers and buds eat raw or boiled. Young shoots can be eaten raw. Hips eat raw , cooked or use for jelly. Add petals to salad. Hips can be dried and crushed for flour. Contains vitamins A, B, C, D, E & P. Calcium, iron, zinc and more.

Cautions: Thorns.

Medicinal: Dried leaves can be infused for a tonic. Use hips & roots for a tea for colds, fever & stomach upsets. Use dried flowers for a tea for heartburn or gargle for sore throats. An infusion of roots, petals, leaves and hips is good for bladder and kidney problems.

Sabal Palm, see Cabbage Palm

Saltwort or Pickleweed

Batis maritima

Where to look: Coastal salt marshes and close to shore.

Identification: Evergreen, low shrub with small, fleshy, finger-shaped green leaves covered with fine hairs which prevent loss from evaporation. Leaves sometimes have a reddish hue.

Edibles: Stems and leaves can be eaten raw – they are salty and crunchy – cooked or pickled. Seeds have nutty taste and can be eaten raw, added to salads, roasted, toasted or ground for flour. White carrot-like roots can be chewed raw.

Cautions: Plant contains oxalic acid – safe in small amounts raw and boiling removes most of it.

Medicinal: Seeds contain antioxidants. Juice is a diuretic.

Sandspur, Coast or Field

Cenchrus spinifex

Where to look: Likes to grow among other grasses in dry, sandy or stony soils with lots of sun.

Identification: Grows up to 30 inches high with clusters of seed heads (burrs) each with many sharp spines that stick to clothes and pierce skin.

Edibles: seeds – raw or part-roasted.

Hold cut stalk over a fire and quickly singe spines off to get to the seeds. If you are not quick the whole stalk will ignite. You can parch and winnow the seeds and use as grain but very labor intensive.

Cautions: Avoid the spines.

Medicinal: None known.

Sarsaparilla, Wild

Aralia nudicaulis

Where to look: Likes moist soils. Understory plant in woodlands.

Straight stem that branches into three each with about five compound ovate, serrated leaflets. Usually three globe-shaped clusters of small greenish-white flowers on separate leafless stalks which develop into dark purple berries. Long, fleshy horizontal creeping rhizomes. Often grows in colonies.

Cautions: Some people may get contact dermatitis from handling roots.

Edibles: Young shoots and leaves are edible raw, boiled or used as flavoring. Aromatic and spicy roots can be cooked, used to make root beer or used to make a mild refreshing tea.

Medicinal: Root tea is diuretic and stimulant and used as a tonic. A poultice of roots for swelling, sprains, sores, minor burns and itchiness.

Saw Palmetto

Serenoa repens

Where to look: Sandy soils in pine uplands, pine woods, prairies and dunes.

Identification: Usually low growing in dense thickets with ground hugging stem and large, stiff, fan-shaped, spikey leaves up to three-feet wide. Leaf stalks have sharp, saw-like edges. Large clusters of white fragrant flowers.

Edibles: Fruit (an acquired taste) and new leaf shoots

Eat young leaves raw in salads or boil as vegetable

Rich in good fatty acids

Cautions: Avoid the sharp leaf stalks.

Medicinal: Extracts from fruit are used to treat prostate disorders. Tincture from fruit used to treat coughs, colds, headaches and chest congestion. Has mild sedative, diuretic and expectorant properties.

Scarlet Rose mallow or swamp hibiscus

Hibiscus coccineus

Where to look: Wet soils and sun. Marshes, river banks and ditches.

Identification: Herbaceous perennial up to seven feet tall with one or many stems. Leaves resemble an open hand with outstretched fingers. It has large, splayed five-petaled scarlet crimson flowers in the upper leaf axils. Each flower lasts for one day but the plant is in bloom for several months.

Edibles: Young leaves, flower buds and flowers can be eaten. Flowers can be soaked to make a refreshing tea.

Cautions: It is a diuretic so make react with some medications.

Medicinal: Antibacterial and astringent. Tea from dried flowers used to improve digestion, lower fevers and for coughs and sore throats.

Seagrape

Coccoloba uvifera

Where to look: Sandy shores, dunes and inland as an ornamental plant.

Identification: Can grow into a small tree with thick, large, alternate, evergreen, leathery and heavily veined round leaves. Leaves are dark shiny green and turn yellow and red before falling off. The smooth bark is mottled with light brown and yellow patches. Green grape-like fruit, each with a single large seed, grows in clusters. Usually grows as shrub along the coast.

Edibles: Ripe purple fruit can be eaten raw. Very astringent when unripe. Ripe berries can be juiced or used for jelly. Rich source of vitamins and minerals.

Cautions: Contains ephedrine. Should be used only after consulting your physician.

Medicinal: Antiviral and antibacterial. Wash of bark, roots and stem used externally on rashes and itches. Poultice of leaves can be applied to stings.

Note: Sea grape is a protected plant in Florida and you cannot forage from it on public land. Fruit can be gathered if you grow it on your own land or from other private land with permission.

Sea Purslane

Sesuvium portulacastrum

Where to look: Coastal dunes and beaches down to the high tide mark.

Identification: An herbaceous perennial with reddish-green branched succulent stems and thick, fleshy opposite, untoothed leaves. Year round it has small pink flowers which only open for a few hours each day. Often grows in dense, spreading clumps.

Edibles: Young stems and leaves are edible raw year round – have a salty tang. They can also be cooked (in two changes of water to remove salt) and pickled.

Cautions: None known.

Medicinal: Antimicrobial. Crushed leaves are applied to cuts and wounds.

Sedges

Where to look: Sedges grow in most environments but are usually found in areas in or near wetlands or with poor soils.

There are more than 5,500 species of sedge with the largest genera being the Carex genus with more than 2,000 species. The important thing is that the seeds of all sedges are edible. Common species in Florida include sawgrass (*Cladium jamaicensis*) and Horned Beakrush (*Rhynchospora inundata*)

Identification: Remember the rhyme: "Sedges have edges, reeds are round and grasses have nodes down to the ground." Sedges have three-sided stems thus the 'edges' and narrow leaves that are spirally arranged in three ranks as opposed to grasses which have stems with nodes and alternate leaves in two ranks. Many sedges, however have names which include the words 'grass' or 'rush',

Edibles: Roots, young shoots, and stems . Roots can be eaten raw, boiled or roasted. Seeds and young leaves can be eaten raw.

Cautions: None known.

Medicinal: Antibacterial. Dried root was chewed to ease stomach and gastric pains.

Skunk vine

Paederia foetida

Where to look: Hardwoods, open woods, mixed and pine forests, sandhill and marshes.

Identification: A misnomer as the plant does not smell that bad although the odor can be intensified after rain. The smell is more vegetable than skunk and greatly magnified if the leaves are crushed releasing sulfur compounds. A woody, thornless vine with slender stems that always twines to the right and can create dense, smothering layers. Leaves are round to lance-shaped with pointed tips and smooth margins. Flowers are small, pink or lilac with red centers.

Cautions: None known.

Edibles: Leaves can be eaten raw or boiled.

Medicinal: Antioxidant, anti-inflammatory and analgesic. Preparation from roots, stem and leaves used to treat skin complaints. Also used to treat rheumatism and gastro-intestinal problems, especially diarrhea.

Smartweed or Dotted Smartweed

Polygonum punctatum

Where to look: Moist and wet habitats.

Identification: Knotty, multi-branched often reddish stem with alternate, long, narrow leaves with pellucid dots. Clusters of small greenish white to pink flowers.

Edibles: Leaves and young stems. Use modestly as seasoning, very peppery.

Cautions: Use sparingly at first and then as you wish if you acquire the taste.

Medicinal: A tincture of all fresh aerial parts as a stimulant, diuretic and antiseptic. An infusion of leaves for coughs and colds.

Southern Dewberry

Rubus trivialis

Where to look: woodland and field margins and disturbed land.

Identification: A sprawling low-growing evergreen vine with woody, tangled stems which often roots at the nodes. Often forms dense thickets. Alternate, palmately compound leaves with three to five leaflets. Single five petaled white to pink flowers on armed pedicel. Clusters of fruit (drupelets) – black when ripe.

Edibles: Fruit can be eaten raw, cooked or used for jam.

Cautions: Thorns.

Medicinal: Astringent. Tea from leaves for diarrhea. Root tea as a mild stimulant. Root infusion for rheumatism and stomach complaints.

Southern Plantain or Dwarf Plantain, see Plantain

Sow Thistle (spiny and common)

Sonchus oleraceus (common sow thistle) and *Sonchus asper* (spiny).

Where to look: Fields, disturbed ground and open spaces.

Identification: Common saw thistle grows tall, is hairless and has sharp-pointed basal lobes that hug the stem. Spiny thistle has spiny leaves that curl at their base.

Edibles: Flower buds, shoots, young leaves, stalks and roots. Scrape thorns from stem, peel and eat raw like celery. Can also be boiled. Roots can be eaten raw (very fibrous) or cooked. Young shoots and leaves can be eaten raw, older leaves are bitter and better cooked or ignored.

Cautions: This is one of the few plants that breaks the rule: "if it has white sap" leave it alone.

Medicinal: Tea from leaves has a calming effect. Tea from roots for colds, coughs and bronchitis. Leaves can be used as a poultice and act as an anti-inflammatory.

Spanish Bayonet

Yucca aloifolia

Where to look: Sandy soil areas – sandhill and pine uplands, woodlands, dunes.

Identification: Tall plant with thick central stem, old stiletto-shaped leaves usually point down while new dark green leaves are clustered at top of the stem and can be three feet in length. White, waxy flowers and fruit, like a purple pickle, is pulpy.

Edibles: Fruit, buds and petals are edible raw. Buds can also be roasted. Peel and boil young flower stalks like asparagus. Fruit can also be boiled by removing seeds and wrapping in foil.

Cautions: Roots contain saponins so best avoided.

Medicinal: Boiled fruit mixed with oil acts as a purgative.

Spanish Moss

Tillandsia usneioides

Where to look: Grows on trees, especially live oaks and bald cypress.

Identification: An angiosperm (not a moss) and a member of the pineapple family, with very long, very narrow leaves that cascade down from tree branches. The flowers are very small and difficult to make out. It is an epiphyte so obtains nutrients and water from the air.

Edibles: Very young green shoots from the growing tip can be eaten raw.

Cautions: None.

Medicinal: Tea from leaves is used to treat fevers and chills. It may have anti-bacterial properties.

Spanish Needles see Beggarticks

Spatterdock or Spadderdock

Nuphar luteum

Also called yellow water lily.

Where to look: Ponds and slow moving water.

Identification: An aquatic perennial with very large oval leaves with a v-notch at the base which grow from the roots (rhizome). Yellow flowers.

Edibles: Seeds can be roasted and ground for flour. Young leaves can be boiled or added to stews. Petals make a refreshing tea. Roots have high levels of tannin and starch and are a food of last resort.

Cautions: Root contains alkaloids so use in moderation (see below).

Medicinal: Leaves are astringent (they stop bleeding) and American Indians used them as bandages and poultices on wound and swellings. Tea from roots used for chills with fever and stomach disorders.

Spiderwort
Tradescantia virginiana

Where to look: edges of woods, thickets and pastures.

Identification: Grows to about 30 inches with succulent stem topped with clusters of three-petaled violet-purple flowers with golden stamen. Long, succulent grass-like leaves.

Edibles: Stems, young shoots, upper leaves, buds and flowers.

Young shoots, leaves and stems can be eaten raw or cooked. Flowers can be eaten raw, added to salads or candied. Cook stems as asparagus.

Cautions: Use in moderation – has laxative properties.

Medicinal: Tea from roots is a laxative. Tea from leaves and flowers treats stomachache. The crushed plant can be used as a poultice for bites and stings. Native Americans used the tough leaves as bandages.

Spotted Beebalm or Horsemint

Monarda punctata

Where to look: well drained but damp soils that get a lot of sun.

Identification: A leafy, showy, aromatic herb that grows in clumps. Square and opposite leaves, both hairy. Can be up to three feet tall. Striking pinkish bracts and small yellow flowers.

Edibles: Infused leaves and flower heads make a refreshing, aromatic tea. Leaves and flowers can be used as flavoring.

Cautions: Use leaves sparingly because of high thymol content

Medicinal: Anti-septic properties. A stronger tea can be used for colds, fevers, colic and stomach aches.

Spring Beauty

Claytonia caroliniana

Where to look: Moist, rich soil woods and clearings. Prefers some shade.

Identification: A small perennial (rarely taller than eight inches) with a single pair of narrow, long lance-like stemless leaves growing from about halfway up the delicate stem. Flowers, on the ends of the stems, have white petals with pinkish streaks.

Cautions: None.

Edibles: Leaves can be eaten raw or cooked as a green. Starch tubers and taproots can be eaten raw but better boiled or roasted.

Medicinal: A decoction of the roots was used to treat childhood convulsions.

Spurge Nettle, Tread Softly or Bull Nettle

Cnidoscolus stimulosus

Where to look: Sandy, well-drained soils, sandhills, woods, scrubs and pastures. If you accidentally step on the plant in bare feet or sandals you will realize why it is called tread softly.

Identification: Not a member of the nettle family. Upright perennial with thick stem with milky sap and alternate, simple green leaves with three to five lobes – like a hand. Terminal clusters of large white flowers with five petals with tubular base. Oval fruit capsule with three seeds. Roots often deep in the ground.

Cautions: Stinging hairs cover the plant and can cause severe skin irritation for several days in some people. Normally stinging sensation wears off after an hour or so. Rubbing plantain leaves on the affected area can relieve the burning,

Edibles: Seeds can be eaten raw. Pick seed pods using thick gloves and place in bag. After a few days the pods will dry and burst open. Seeds can be eaten raw but are best roasted. Roots (tubers) can be cooked and mashed as potato. Dig down about a foot several inches from the side of plant and then use your hands to locate and extract the tuber, avoid contact with all above ground parts.

Medicinal: Root is diuretic. American Indians used the milky sap for herbal remedies.

Sweet Gum

Liquidambar styraciflua

Where to look: moist woods, hydric habitats.

Identification: Member of the witch-hazel family. Very tall, straight, deciduous tree (up to 150 feet) with rough grayish-bark and star-shaped, shiny leaves with five to seven pointed lobes. Globular fruits with projecting spikes.

Edibles: Sap and seeds. Hardened resin (balsam) was used by settlers as an early chewing gum. Sap is not sweet but not as bitter as the black gum.

Cautions: None

Medicinal: Fruit and seeds contain shishimic acid, a natural Tamiflu, used to treat flu. It has antiseptic, antimicrobial, anti-inflammatory and expectorant properties. Resin can be chewed for colds, sore throats and diarrhea and used externally for sores, wounds and skin problems. Inner bark was boiled and used to treat diarrhea and dysentery. Leaves are aromatic when crushed.

Switchcane, Giant Cane or Large Cane

Arundinaria gigantea

Where to look: River banks, swamps and marshes, low lying ground.

Identification: Tall, woody, bamboo-like plant with hollow stems and long, flat, grass-like leaves. Often grows in dense thickets. Flowers in racemes with clusters of flattened spikelets bearing seeds.

Edibles: Young shoots are edible raw with a nutty taste and can be cooked. Seeds can be used as flour.

Cautions: Plant can be attacked by ergot, a toxic fungus which takes the place of some of the seeds. Affected areas may vary in color from pink to black. If plant looks diseased, avoid it.

Medicinal: Cathartic. A decoction of crushed roots used to stimulate the kidneys and as a tonic.

Sword fern or Tuber Ladder Fern

Nephrolepis cordifolia

Where to look: On the ground in shady woods and wood margins. Also grows as an epiphyte, especially on palms in moist hammocks.

Identification: Erect, dull green fronds up to three feet high with up to 100 oblong leaflets (pinnae) on each side of the spine (rachis). Large pea-like brown tubers on roots.

Edibles: Tubers on roots are water storage organs and good source of carbs.   Eat crunchy raw, slow roast or dry.

Cautions: None known.

Medicinal: Antibacterial and antifungal. Root tea for stomach upsets. Decoction of fresh fronds for fever and colds.

Turkey Tail (fungi)
Trametes versicolor

Where to look: In woods on fallen, dead and rotting trees, stumps and large branches.

Identification: This is an unmistakable fan-shaped mushroom with reddish, brown and black concentric bands resembling a male turkey's tail. It has a fuzzy cap and small pores which are clearly visible. It is the most common polypore and a member of the Trametes genus. It is often called shelf or bracket fungi because of the way it grows on dead fallen wood, especially oaks.

Edibles: Fruiting body of young mushrooms with clean white pore underside (with a little flex in them as they become rigid and dry when old). Very young mushrooms can be eaten raw but it is like chewing a piece of leather with very little flavor. They can be slowly boiled in milk to make them a little more palatable. They can be dried (pores side up), ground and used as a tea.

Cautions: None known.

Medicinal: Infuse in boiling water for a soothing tea. Anti-tumor, anti-microbial, immunomodulating, anti-oxidant, anti-malarial.

Research suggests that parts of the mushroom yielding polysaccharide-K (PSK) may help in the fight against cancer.

Usnea, Oak Moss or Old Man's Beard

Usnea barbata

Where to look: Usnea is an epiphytic lichen that grows on dead or dying wood at the tops of trees, especially oaks. Collect straight after storm or high winds when branches blown down.

Identification: A pale green, gray lichen with stems covered in what look like small bristles of a beard. Definitive identification is to gently pull the stem apart and you should see a white sap that has some elasticity.

Edibles: Whole plant. High in vitamin C. Eat raw in small quantities or infuse for tea with two changes of water.

Cautions: Should be used in moderation.

Medicinal: Strong antiseptic, antifungal, antibiotic and antiviral properties. Can be packed in wounds to speed healing and prevent infection. As an antifungal poultice to treat athlete's foot. Tea is used as a tonic and for colds and sore throats. Can be used as a mouthwash for mouth infections and sores.

Violet, Common Blue or Wooly Blue Violet

Viola sororia

Where to look: Moist areas with shade.

Identification: A small herbaceous, perennial plant with broad, heart-shaped leaves and five-petaled blue purple (sometimes white) flowers on separate stems growing from the root. Lower petals veined.

Edibles: Flowers, leaves and root. Leaves can be eaten raw (best mixed with other greens as they have little flavor) or cooked as greens or as a soup thickener. Dried leaves can be used as a tea. Flowers can be eaten raw, added to salads or desserts. All members of the viola family are edible. Rich in vitamins A and C.

Cautions: None known.

Medicinal: Expectorant and laxative. Can be used as soothing agent, for headaches and as mild expectorant. Used to make tea or syrup. Leaf poultice used for headaches. Root poultice used for boils and sores.

Wapato, Broad-Leaved Arrowhead or Duck Potatoes, see Arrowhead

Water hyacinth (invasive)

Eichhornia crassipes

Where to look: Still or slow moving water.

Identification: Prolific floating perennial plant (population can double in two weeks). Has erect spike of six lobed blue-purple flowers – one petal has a yellow dot - and a floating rosette of broad, thick, glossy, ovate leaves. Leaf stalks are bulbous at the base.

Edibles: Carotene rich. Young leaves, flowers and spongy leafstalks from clean waters only (they absorb pollutants). Leaves and young leaf stalks eat raw or cooked – boiled or fried. Flowers boiled, spongy stem bases – fried.

Cautions: Eating parts of the plant – raw or cooked - can cause itching in some people. Use caution when trying for the first time.

Medicinal: Leaf petioles are eaten to treat diarrhea.

Water Hyssop

Bacopa Monnieri

Where to look: Wetlands, marshes. Can tolerate semi-brackish water.

Identification: A small creeping perennial herb with multiple branches and spatula-shaped succulent leaves. Small white flowers with four or five petals which may have purple tips.

Cautions: Should be avoided if pregnant and consult your medical profession if you are on medication.

Edibles: Leaves –pickled or as tea, very bitter (add honey).

Medicinal: Antioxidant and highly astringent. Tisane from dried leaves good for memory function, cramming for exams, stress and anxiety. A decoction of fresh or dried leaves for bronchitis. A decoction of leaves and petals used externally on scalp is said to encourage hair growth. It can also be used on skin irritations and minor cuts. A poultice of fresh leaves for wounds to aid healing and prevent infection. Lot of research currently underway to see if the plant can be used to treat patients with dementia.

Water Cress, Common

Nasturtium officinale

Where to look: Running water.

Identification: Floating, creeping fast-growing aquatic perennial plant with hollow stems, clusters of tiny white and pepper-tasting green flowers and pinnately compounded leaves with pairs of oblong leaflets. Can form dense mats.

Edibles: All aerial parts. Can be eaten raw or cooked as greens or added to soups. Leaves are more bitter after flowering. Rich in vitamins A, B, C and E and minerals iron, calcium, iodine and folic acid..

Cautions: Wash leaves thoroughly. Do not collect from polluted waterways or in areas where livestock grazes.

Medicinal: Diuretic, expectorant and mild stimulant. Soup from leaves used for sore or swollen gums and mouth ulcers. Infusion of leaves used externally for dermatitis, eczema, arthritis and rheumatism pains. Tea from fresh leaves is a diuretic.

Water Lettuce

Pistia stratiotes

Where to look: Wetlands, still and slow moving water.

Identification: Floating rosette of large, dull green, thick, spongy, veined and ridged hairy leaves, broad at the tip and with no leaf stem. Long trailing roots. Inconspicuous flowering spathes usually hidden. Can form dense mats. Looks like an open head of lettuce.

Edibles: Young leaves – wash thoroughly and boil.

Cautions: Contains large amounts of calcium oxalate. Don't eat raw.

Medicinal: Diuretic, antidiabetic, antifungal and antimicrobial. Poultice of crushed leaves for boils, wounds, swellings and skin infections. Infusion of leaves has been used for diabetes.

Wax Myrtle, Miracle bush or Southern Bayberry

Myrica cerifera

Where to look: swamps and thickets but grows in most habitats.

Identification: Evergreen, dense-foliaged shrub or small tree with long, alternate, leathery, aromatic, oblong to lance-shaped leaves toothed towards the tip. Resin glands visible as spots on upper and underside. Clusters of small, waxy, berrylike fruit (nutlets).

Edibles: Leaves can be used as a flavoring instead of bay leaves. Berries can be eaten raw, cooked and added to season game. Soak berries in water and the oil floats to the surface

Cautions: Use in moderation.

Medicinal: Astringent, anti-inflammatory, antibacterial and diuretic. Root tea used as an astringent and emetic. Leaf tea used for fevers and applied externally to reduce itching. Juice from leaves and berries acts as insect repellent. Wood smoke has same effect

Waxy fruit used to be used to produce candles.

White Clover

Trifolium repens

Where to look: Meadows, pastures, fields, roadsides and lawns.

Identification: A low growing perennial. Leaflets in threes (like shamrocks) often have 'V' markings. Leaves and round heads of white flowers grow on separate stalks from creeping runners. Often grows in dense clumps.

Edibles: Protein rich. Leaves, flowers and seed pods and roots. Leaves and flowers can be eaten raw but best soaked first or cooked. Cooks like spinach. Flowers and seed pods can be dried and ground for flour. Roots can be roasted.

Cautions: Don't overindulge on raw leaves.

Medicinal: Antioxidant. Tea from dried flowers for an invigorating tea and for rheumatic pains. Leaf tea for colds and fevers. Tincture of flowers and leaves applied externally for sores, cuts and abrasions.

Wild Balsam Pear or Balsam Melon, Bitter Melon or Bitter Gourd

Momordica charantia

Where to look: Disturbed areas hedgerows, fences – anywhere it can climb.

Identification: Herbaceous vine with climbing tendrils and long stalked, simple, alternate leaves and yellow flowers from leaf axils. Produces 'warty' gourds which turn from green to orange when fully ripe. The gourds then bursts open to expose the seeds and their red aril covering.

Edibles: Young fruit while still green– an acquired taste but do not eat seeds. Rich in potassium and vitamins. Yellow and orange rind and seeds of older fruit are toxic. Young leaves and flowers can be boiled.

Cautions: Not to be consumed if pregnant. Use in moderation - can cause stomach upset. Avoid ripe fruit and do not eat seeds.

Medicinal: Scientific studies suggest it may benefit diabetics as it can have a hypoglycemic effect.

Wild Lettuce or Grassleaf lettuce

Lactuca graminifolia

Where to look: Fields and woodlands.

Identification: Tall (up to three feet) leafy plant with alternate, dandelion-like, thin, spatula-shaped, deeply lobed leaves. Has panicles of light purple stellate flowers.

Edibles: Rich in vitamins and minerals although bitter. Young shoots and leaves can be eaten raw but are bitter. Older leaves should be boiled in at least two changes of water.

Cautions: Sap may cause contact dermatitis or allergic reaction.

Medicinal: Mild sedative and diuretic. Tea from leaves used as a pain reliever, mild sedative and for insomnia.

Wild Radish or Jointed Charlock

Raphanus raphanistrum

Where to look: Fields, pastures, roadsides, open, waste and disturbed ground.

Identification: Starts as a rosette of leaves from which the flower stem develops. Grows to about four feet with branching in the top half. Lower large, fleshy leaves are ovate, deeply lobed and hairy, upper leaves are smaller, oblong and toothed. Flowers are single with four-petals shaped like a cross and can vary in color from white to yellow to purple and may have violet veins. The seed pods, under the flowers, are segmented with four to twelve seeds.

Edibles: Leaves, flower buds and growing tips can be eaten raw or cooked. They freeze well. Flowers can be added to salads. Young seedpods can be eaten raw. Seeds can be eaten raw, cooked or ground and used as a mustard-like condiment. Peeled roots can be boiled.

Cautions: May cause stomach upsets in some people.

Medicinal: Antirheumatic. Tea from roots used for stomach upsets. Poultice from leaves for skin irritations.

Wild Rice

Zizania aquatica

Where to look: Shallow waters with muddy or sandy bottoms.

Identification: Grows in clumps in the water with lance-like leaves and stalks that can be up to ten feet above the water.

Edibles: Rich in protein, carbs, minerals and vitamins. Best to harvest from a boat. Bend the stalks over a sheet and tap them with a stick. If the grain is ripe it will fall onto the sheet. Ripe seeds vary in color from green to brown. Dry, winnow and grind into flour.

Cautions: Look for signs of ergot, a fungus that attacks grasses and is dangerous if ingested. Look for pink or purplish fungi among the seeds.

Medicinal: Unknown.

Wild Taro, Dasheen or Elephant Ears

Colocasia esculenta

Where to look: Waterways, shorelines and moist soils.

Identification: An invasive that grows quickly and smothers other vegetation. Has large arrowhead or elephant-earlike, dark green leaves on long stalks and an inflorescence on a fleshy stalk, partly encased in a yellow spathe. Petioles may be purplish. Top of the stalk is densely covered with tiny flowers.

Edibles: Young leaves, soaked overnight and then boiled. Roots should also be soaked overnight and then roasted.

Cautions: Contains calcium oxalate. Don't eat raw.

Medicinal: Antirheumatic, diuretic and laxative. Juice from leaves used as styptic.

Willow or **Coastal Plain Willow**

Salix caroliniana

Where to look: Wetlands, forested wetlands, pond, river and lake margins.

Identification: Large shrub or small tree with short trunk, often leaning, and spreading, open crown. The leaves are long (up to eight inches), alternate, simple narrow, and dark green and sharp-tipped with paler undersides. It has greenish yellow flowers (catkins) with air-borne seeds.

Edibles: Young twigs, growing tips, inner bark. Twigs and inner bark are high in vitamin C and very bitter but can be eaten raw but are best boiled to reduce the bitterness. Inner bark can be dried, ground and used as flour.

Cautions: None known.

Medicinal: Chew young twigs to cure headaches. Contains Salicin, a natural aspirin-like compound. Tea made from infused bark combats fever, colds and sore throats and was used by American Indians to thin blood. Chewing young twigs relieves toothache. Stronger tea used to induce vomiting.

Winged Sumac   or Dwarf Sumac

Rhus copallinum

Where to look: Woods and clearings with well drained soils.

Identification: A shrub or small tree with drooping branches and compound, shiny dark green foliage which turns to orange in the fall. Long leaves with numerous (up to thirty) toothless leaflets and a noticeable wing along the midrib. Tiny, green-yellow flowers, borne on terminal panicles, are replaced by clusters of red hairy, berries which can stay on the tree for weeks.

Edibles: Soak berries and strain before drinking for a refreshing drink.

Cautions: None known. This species of sumac is not in the same family as poison ivy and poison oak.

Medicinal: Wash from bark for blisters and skin irritations. Tea from roots was used to treat dysentery and berries can be chewed for sores and ulcers in the mouth.

Winged yam, Purple Yam and Water Yam

Dioscorea alata

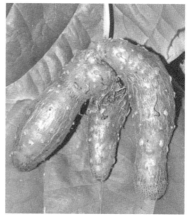

Where to look: Wood margins, fences and hedgerows – pretty much anywhere it can climb.

Identification: A climbing vine with thick, squarish stem with wide ridges (wings) and pairs of opposite, large, arrow-shaped leaves with marked veins. The vine spirals upwards from left to right (what Green Deane calls the 'Z' twist). The bulbils (fruit) are dark brown to black and look like small shriveled sausages. The tuberous roots can be massive (in old plants they can be well over 100 lbs).

Edibles: Eat young roots as potato - roast or boil – and slice, dry and grind older roots for flour. Roots have high carb (mostly starch) content.

Peel, cut up and boil as potatoes. Pound older roots into sticky dough or cut into slices then parboil and dry in sun before grinding.

Cautions: Distinguishable from air potatoes by square stems and color of bulbils. Overindulgence can cause diarrhea.

Medicinal: Diuretic and laxative. Root tea for fever.

Wood Ear or Tree Ear Mushroom

Auricularia auricular-judae

Where to look: Fallen dead and living wood and tree stumps.

Identification: Distinctive floppy ear or cup shape. Outer surface is veined, tan-brown with purple tints and often covered in tiny, grey hairs. Inner surface is grey brown. Younger specimens tend to be smooth and the outer surface wrinkles with age. It gets darker – almost black - as it ages. Stalk is very small or non-existent. Spores underneath are white. Can be solitary or in groups.

Edibles: Young fruit body – always slow cooked. Soft, rubbery-like texture best used in soups and stews. Can be dried and ground and added to cooking dishes.

Cautions: None known.

Medicinal: Astringent and anticoagulant and may have cholesterol-lowering properties. As a tea or soup for sore throats, coughs and colds. As a poultice for eye irritations

Wood Sorrel

Violet wood-sorrel *Oxalis violaceae* and Yellow wood sorrel *oxalis stricta*

Where to look: Open, damp woodlands, shaded slopes and prairies.

Identification: Perennial rarely more than six inches high. Both have shamrock leaves with three heart shaped leaflets. The violet wood sorrel has showy pink-purple bell shaped flowers with five petals while the yellow wood sorrel has pale yellow flowers.

Edibles: Always sharp flavor (oxalis is derived from the Greek word for sour) but young leaves can be added to salads, cooked as a potherb (which also reduces levels of oxalic acid) or used for a refreshing drink. The flowers can be eaten raw or used to garnish salads, and the root bulbs can be eaten raw or cooked.

Cautions: Contain oxalic acid and potassium oxalate – use in moderation and not for prolonged periods especially if you suffer from arthritis, gout or rheumatism.

Medicinal: Diuretic. Leaves and flowers soaked in cold water used to stop vomiting.

Yarrow

Achillea millefolium

Where to look: Grasslands, open woods and forests, roadsides and disturbed areas.

Identification: An erect, herbaceous scented perennial with one or more stems. Feather-like leaves are evenly spaced along the stems and are arranged spirally. Inflorescence clusters at the top of the stems have white flowers (occasionally pink) with five petal-like rays with toothed tips, and are flat topped.

Edibles: Cook young leaves like spinach or add to soups. Leaves can also be dried and used as a herb because of their sweet but slightly bitter flavor.

Cautions: Should not be used over prolonged periods. Some people may suffer an allergic reaction from contact with or eating the plant.

Medicinal: Astringent, diuretic, tonic and mild stimulant. The leaves can be used as a poultice to stop bleeding which is why another name for this plant is woundwort. A tea made from the leaves and flowers is an anti-inflammatory and diuretic. A tea from the leaves alone overcomes insomnia. A wash made from the leaves can be used to treat minor burns, stings, bites and rashes. Native Americans dried and crushed the leaves and snorted them like snuff to relieve headaches. They also chewed the leaves for toothache.

Yaupon Holly, see Holly

Yucca, see Adam's Needle

Edible Critters

If it moves, crawls, swims or flies – eat it.

Crustaceans/Bivalves

Clams

All edible

Raw, steam, boil or bake

Add to soups and stews

Oysters

All edible

Raw, steam, boil or bake

Crabs

Body and claw meat

All crabs are edible

Crawfish, salt and freshwater

Body

Steam, boil or bake

Fish

All species

All edible

Can be eaten raw

Eat fresh as meat deteriorates quickly

Reptiles

Alligator

All meat

Tail has most flavor, body meat darker

All turtles

All meat and eggs

Note: Gopher Tortoise is a land turtle and protected.

All lizards/skinks

All species are edible

Remove head, gut and roast

Skewer smaller prey whole and roast

All Snakes

All species are edible

Remove head, gut and roast

Can be eaten raw

Birds

All birds

All birds and eggs are edible

Remove feathers, entrails, boil or roast.

Skin is very rich in nutrients

Animals

Armadillo

All meat is edible

Remove armor, gut, cut into chunks

Best roasted

Hog - wild

All meat is edible

Skin, gut and roast

Mice

All meat is edible

Skin, gut and roast on skewer

Meat rich in protein

Rabbit

All meat is edible

Skin, gut and roast, stew or braise

Raccoon

All meat is edible

Skin, gut, tenderize by boiling then roast

Rat

All meat is edible

Skin, gut and roast or grill

Tastes like pork

Skunk

All meat is edible

Skin, gut, remove scent sac intact and roast

Squirrel

All meat is edible

Skin, gut and roast, boil or stew.

Insects

While there is reluctance in the west to eat insects they are an essential food source in many parts of the world and often considered great delicacies. Insects are also a rich source of proteins, amino and fatty acids, micronutrients and calories. The raw yellow mealworm larva, common in the U.S. provides 206 calories per 100 grams of fresh weight. The raw Australian plague locust has almost 500 calories per 100 grams of fresh weight.

Ants, Bees and wasps
Hymenoptera

Adults, pupae, larvae and eggs may have a protein content up to 77 percent.

Black beetles

All edible

Beetles (Coleoptera) account for about 40% of all known insect species. Protein content can be as high as 66 percent.

Larvae of Dytiscidae, Gyrinidae and Hydrophilidae are edible

Butterflies and Moths
Lepidoptera

Caterpillars are among the world's most diverse groups of edible insects and are valuable sources of protein and other micronutrients. Pupae and larvae can have protein content as high as 68 percent.

Mostly the larvae are eaten but many butterflies and moths are edible after removing wings and legs.

Witchetty grubs, the larvae of cossid moth, is a staple desert food of the Australian aborigines. It can be eaten raw (best to bite the head off first) and has an almond-like taste. When fried the skin tastes like the skin of roasted chicken while the inside has an almost peanut-butter taste.

Cicadas, leafhoppers and scale insects
Homoptera

Adults, larvae and eggs can have a protein content as high as 57 percent.

Cicadas have asparagus flavor.

Crickets, grasshoppers and locusts
Orthoptera

Adults and nymphs can have a protein content as high as 65 percent.

Eat raw or boiled.

Cockroaches/palmetto bugs

Eat raw, fried or boiled.

Roaches found in or near houses may contain bacteria so should be eaten cooked. High in protein – pound for pound five times more protein than beef.

Termites
Isoptera

Termites are considered a delicacy in many parts of the world. They are eaten both as main and side dishes, and as snack foods after they have been de-winged, fried and sun-dried. Termites are rich in protein, fatty acids and other micronutrients. Fried or dried termites are almost 40 percent protein.

Larvae and adults can be eaten raw, but adults best cooked.

When you bite into a termite larva it is like getting a blast of pepper in your mouth.

True Bugs
Heteroptera, suborder of Hemiptera

Adults and larvae can have a protein content as high as 74 percent.

Mexican 'caviar' *ahuahutle* comes from the eggs of several species of aquatic Hemiptera.

Worms

Larvae of many species are edible including mealworm (Tenebrionidae) and superworm (Zophobas morio).

Trapping

Trap birds, animals and fish, clean and eat as soon as possible.

Roast young birds, boil old birds

Fish can be wrapped in leaves, baked in embers or stewed

Many creatures can be eaten raw – snakes (not the head), fish and insects

Boil shellfish and eat, boil turtles until the shell comes off and then roast

Gut reptiles and amphibians and roast in fire embers, small lizards can be cooked on a stick over the fire (skin frogs first)

Footnote. It really does taste like chicken!

Taste – because of muscle composition and density

Small critters (up to the size of a small dog) really do tend to taste like chicken

Medium size critters (up the size of a large dog) tend to taste like pork

Large critters tend to taste like beef

Notes.

Notes.

Notes.

About the authors

Don Philpott has been writing and experiencing the great outdoors for more than 50 years. He has backpacked, climbed, canoed, ridden and skied throughout Europe, North America, Africa, Asia, the Arctic, Australia and New Zealand. He cofounded Footloose, the first environmental outdoors magazine in the UK in the 1970's and has written more than 60 books on camping, campfire cooking, travel, survival and the great outdoors. He is an instructor with the University of Florida's Florida Master Naturalist program, a Certified Interpretive Guide and member of the National Association for Interpretation. As a member of the Wekiva Wilderness Trust and a volunteer at Wekiwa Springs State Park, he helps run interpretive programs and guided walks and regularly conducts edible Florida and basic survival classes. He also serves on the Board of Friends of Florida State Parks Inc.

Noreen Corle Engstrom fell in love with all things outdoors when just a child. As a teenager she tramped the woods and fields near her home collecting wildflowers, butterflies and other things that caught her fancy. She harvested, pressed and dried a large collection of local wildflowers, searching out their identities in a 1912 edition of Field Book of American Wild Flowers by F. Schuyler Mathews. Since then she has camped, hiked, canoed and kayaked many North American wild places. She is a Florida Master Naturalist and a member of the Florida Wildflower Foundation. While taking the Florida Master Naturalist Program she began a project of photographing and identifying the wild flowers of the Wekiva River Basin. This project has grown to include wildflowers wherever she finds them, throughout Florida, and from California to Maine, Florida to Washington State. Since most edible and medicinal plants flower, her project fits nicely into this book. She is a member of the Wekiva Wilderness Trust and a volunteer at Wekiwa Springs State Park where she conducts interpretive walks for children and adults and serves as River Patrol and Trail Guide.